MW00713414

TREATISE ON GRACE

TREATISE ON GRACE

and other posthumously published writings

by

Jonathan Edwards

Edited, with an Introduction

by

PAUL HELM

JAMES CLARKE & CO. LTD.

Cambridge & London

This edition first published 1971

Introduction © by Paul Helm.

Published by
James Clarke & Co. Ltd.,
7 All Saints Passage, Cambridge
and distributed by
Trade Counter Ltd
11-14 Stanhope Mews West
Kensington, S.W.7

Printed in Great Britain by
Latimer Trend & Co. Ltd., Whitstable

CONTENTS

1 Tim. 1.7 *Now unto the King eternal, immortal, invisible, the only wise God, be honour and glory for ever and ever.* As I read the words, there came into my soul, and was as it were diffused through it, a sense of the glory of the divine Being; a new sense, quite different from anything I ever experienced before.

EDWARDS, *Personal Narrative.*

EDITOR'S NOTE

THE three items republished here all first appeared separately more than sixty years ago, but are not included in any edition of Edwards' *Works*. Despite the fact that Yale University Press is engaged in publishing a standard edition of all Edwards' writings (two volumes, *Freedom of the Will* and *Religious Affections*, have so far appeared) it is believed to be worth while publishing these pieces together because of their extreme rarity, and the fact that they together form a unity of certain important themes not handled elsewhere at any length by Edwards. In the Introduction a short account of the background of each item is given, and a sketch is made of some of the connections between the views that Edwards propounds here, and his other, better-known works. Despite recent claims to the contrary it is clear that Edwards was working quite explicitly within the framework of the Reformed Faith that he inherited. It is also clear that his work was a remarkable combination of religious devotion and intellectual fertility. Convinced as he was that God had spoken clearly and finally in the Bible, his career was an attempt, not without tragedy, to respond to that revelation with heart and mind. For this reason he would hardly have recognized the post-Kantian world which most Protestants live in today. Yet modern Protestantism— anthropocentric, moral and chronically unsure—could do worse than heed Edwards' testimony to a God who has declared His grace in Scripture and who in every generation imparts His Spirit to men.

In preparing the texts no attempt has been made to amend Edwards' punctuation, spelling, or style. However in the interests of readability his lavish and inconsistent use of capitals has been standardized, and many of the contractions he used, particularly for persons of the Trinity, expanded. (This applies mainly to the *Essay on the Trinity*.) Mistakes in Bible references and quotations have been rectified as far as possible. In the case of the *Treatise on*

Grace two paragraphs which A. B. Grosart, the original editor, placed in footnotes on the grounds that they interrupted the argument have been reinserted in the main text. Some of the previous editors' footnotes have been retained; those by the present editor have been marked '—H'. Words within square brackets are either the additions of the original editors, or indicate illegibilities or later insertions by Edwards.

Thanks are due to the staff of the Harold Cohen Library, University of Liverpool and to Mr. A. Douglas Millard of Messrs. James Clarke for their help in tracing books and obtaining photocopies.

PAUL HELM

INTRODUCTION

WHEN Jonathan Edwards died of a smallpox vaccination on 22nd March 1758, two months after moving to Princeton as its President, he left a mass of manuscript material, including over a thousand sermons and pieces in various stages of completion. One of his major theological works, *The Great Christian Doctrine of Original Sin Defended*, was on its way through the press. Books for which Edwards has become famous, such as *The History of Redemption* (1774), *The End for which God created the World*, *The Nature of True Virtue* (1765) were published posthumously, as were some of his sermons and extracts from his voluminous *Miscellanies* which were in effect his theological and philosophical notebooks. Since the various editions of Edwards' *Works* published in the nineteenth century, manuscript items have continued to appear, making quite a large body of material in print but not included in his *Works*, and not readily available. The largest of these items is *Charity and Its Fruits*, sermons on *I Corinthians 11*, edited by his great-grandson Tryon Edwards and published in 1852.[1] The three reprinted here, though slighter, are not less important for understanding Edwards.

Treatise on Grace

In 1854 Alexander B. Grosart was commissioned to prepare a new edition of Edwards' writings and was given access to the mass of his manuscripts. This edition never appeared, because, according to Faust and Johnson, Grosart quarrelled with the American executors of Edwards' estate over his removal of material to Scotland.[2] Extracts from this material were privately printed by

---

[1] This has been republished (London 1969).

[2] C. H. Faust and T. H. Johnson, *Jonathan Edwards: Representative Selections*, revised edition, New York 1962, p. 424.

him in 1865, in an edition of only three hundred copies, as *Selections from the Unpublished Writings of Jonathan Edwards of America*. The *Treatise on Grace* was the chief item in this selection, which besides included some annotations on the Bible, sermons and letters. Grosart writes of the *Treatise*, 'This Manuscript was found by itself carefully placed within folds of thick paper, and tied up with a silk ribbon. It proved to be arranged into chapters and sections, all paged; and, in short, precisely as now printed . . . there can be no doubt that the Manuscript was intended for publication.'[1] There is no clear indication when it was written though A. V. G. Allen believes that both it and the *Observations* came after 1752.[2]

When a search was made at the turn of this century for the documents that Grosart took from America, nothing was found. Faust and Johnson hazard that Grosart did not in fact possess documents of any great interest, but the impression given in his Introduction to the *Selections* is the reverse of this. 'I have personally transcribed from the original MSS now in my possession, the contents of the present volume'. 'I possess already priceless and hitherto unknown materials for a worthy Biography.'[3]

It is not clear, therefore, just what manuscripts Grosart took to Scotland and how many, if any, he returned. Harvey Townsend claimed that Grosart 'never rendered a satisfactory accounting for some of them'. If so, Grosart certainly merits Townsend's description of him as 'irresponsible'.[4] So it is not clear where, if anywhere, the autograph of the *Treatise on Grace* is. It is not mentioned as being in either of the two principal collections of Edwards' manuscripts, at Yale and Andover-Newton Theological Seminary.

---

[1] *Selections*, p. 12.
[2] A. V. G. Allen, *Jonathan Edwards*, Edinburgh 1889, p. 346.
[3] *Selections*, pp. 11, 15.
[4] *The Philosophy of Jonathan Edwards from his Private Notebooks*, ed. Harvey G. Townsend, Eugene, Oregon 1955, p. xi.

Observations Concerning the Scripture Economy of the Trinity and the Covenant of Redemption

This, the smallest of the three items, is in effect a section (No. 1062) from a copy of Edwards' *Miscellanies*, pages 573–88 of a manuscript book prepared for publication by Edwards' son. It was published by E. C. Smyth in 1880, with an introduction and appendices. Smyth believed it to be the unpublished essay of Edwards on the Trinity referred to by Horace Bushnell and O. W. Holmes (see p. 4). A volume of Edwards' *Miscellaneous Observations* copied by his son was published in Edinburgh in 1793 by Edwards' friend and correspondent John Erskine, but for some reason the section republished by Professor Smyth was omitted by Jonathan Edwards junior and remained in America. Smyth could give no explanation of the decision to hold back the section, except that it was perhaps not considered by Edwards' son to be of sufficient interest at the time. Another still shorter entry of Edwards on the Trinity was reprinted by Smyth in 1904 in *Exercises Commemorating the Two-Hundredth Anniversary of the Birth of Jonathan Edwards*, Appendix I, pp. 8–16, and is reprinted in Harvey Townsend ed. *The Philosophy of Jonathan Edwards*, pp. 252–61. Townsend does not mention this section as forming part of the *Miscellanies* when he estimates that as much as three-quarters of the *Miscellanies* have been published in more-or-less adequate texts. Pending the publication of the standard edition of Edwards' *Miscellanies*[1] Townsend's volume, a carefully edited selection under subject headings derived from Edwards' own index, is invaluable.

Professor Smyth provided a very lengthy Appendix to the *Observations*, consisting mainly of further extracts from the unpublished *Miscellanies* in support and elucidation of the newly-published text. Only those extracts that serve to underline the extent of Edwards' commitment to covenant theology (for the significance of this commitment see below) have been retained.

[1] Due to be published by Yale University Press, edited by Professor Thomas Schafer.

An Essay on the Trinity

This appeared in 1903, edited by G. P. Fisher (1827–1909), who was for many years Professor of Ecclesiastical History at Yale. He assumes that the *Essay* was in fact the 'treatise' mentioned by Horace Bushnell in 1851[1], as providing an '*a priori* argument for the Trinity' and also mentioned by O. W. Holmes. Holmes had written:

> The writer is informed on unquestionable authority that there is or was in existence a manuscript of Edwards in which his views appear to have undergone a great change in the direction of Arianism, or of Sabellianism, which is an old-fashioned Unitarianism, or at any rate show a defection from his former standard of orthodoxy, and which its custodians, thinking it best to be wise as serpents in order that they might continue harmless as doves, have considered it their duty to withold from the public. If any of our friends at Andover can inform us what are the facts about this manuscript, such information would be gratefully received by many enquirers, who would be rejoiced to know that so able and so good a man lived to be emancipated from the worse than heathen conceptions which had so long enchained his powerful, but crippled understanding.[2]

Fisher believed that the item referred to was the *Essay* and that Professor Smyth was mistaken in thinking that it referred to the fragment of Edwards that he published, on account of the fact that Bushnell refers to it as a 'treatise', which the *Observations* published by Smyth certainly was not. In the second of two articles in *Bibliotheca Sacra* in 1881 Professor E. A. Park had referred to an 'early metaphysical and scholastic but utterly orthodox argument on the Trinity' which 'has been mislaid and cannot yet be found'. The Edwards family had in fact put this in the hands of Professor Park who was hoping to write a biography of Edwards. On his death the manuscripts went to Yale.

[1] *Christ in Theology*, p. vi.
[2] *Pages from an Old Volume of Life*, p.396 (vol. viii of the Riverside Edition of the *Writings of O. W. Holmes*, London 1891).

Why was it not printed sooner than 1903? Fisher hazards the guess that it was on account of Edwards' upholding of the Nicene doctrine of the eternal generation of the Son of God which nine-teenth-century New England theology had abandoned and derided. It would have been something of an embarrassment to them to have had the orthodox view defended by someone who was on all hands regarded as the founder of their school. On this view not heterodoxy, but orthodoxy, prevented its earlier publication. However this may be, it is clear that the contents of the *Essay* do nothing to justify the rather back-handed remarks of Holmes. The most obvious reason why Edwards did not publish this himself, along with the *Treatise on Grace*, is that he was prevented by his sudden death. Writing to the Princeton trustees in 1757 he mentions his plans for writing on other aspects of the Arminian controversy, for writing a *History of the Work of Redemption*, and a *Harmony of the Old and New Testaments*. He goes on, 'I have also many other things in hand, in some of which I have made great progress, which I will not trouble you with an account of. Some of these things, if Divine Providence favour, I should be willing to attempt a publication of.'[1]

The date of the composition of the *Essay* is not known, but it is clear from alterations to the draft that it was composed over a considerable number of years, and in any case could not have been finished (assuming Edwards had finished it, in content if not in style) before 1727, for the simple reason that in it Edwards refers to John Hurrion's *Christ Crucified* which was not published until then. The *Essay* has not been reprinted since 1903, though fragments of it appear in Faust and Johnson's *Representative Selections*.

II THEOLOGICAL

In introducing the themes dealt with by Edwards in these writings it will be convenient to start with his concept of divine grace, which can be regarded as a pivotal notion of his theology.

---

[1] *Works*, ed. Hickman, London 1840, vol. i, p. ccxvii. (All references to Edwards' *Works* are to this edition).

Edwards believed that the Bible taught one unified theme, trinitarian in scope, comprising a revelation of God's redemptive grace. This same belief had been articulated by Edwards' Puritan forebears in terms of covenant theology; according to this scheme God the Father had covenanted with the Son (as the head and representative of the church) to redeem the church through the Son's propitiatory sacrifice, and the Holy Spirit was conceived of as the agency of application of the 'benefits' or 'fruits' of Christ's death to the elect—bringing them to repentance and saving faith, granting them the grace of adoption and assurance, and progressively sanctifying them. Theologians such as Ames, Perkins and Preston were prominent 'covenant theologians' in Britain, and Turretine and Witsius on the continent, but its influence was pervasive in Reformed circles in the seventeenth century, and found classic expression in such documents as the *Westminster Confession of Faith*.

At two points in these re-published writings Edwards seems to modify this covenant doctrine. (*Essay*, p. 123–4; *Treatise*, p. 68). In each case he stresses that the common way of expressing the Holy Spirit's part in the covenant does not do full justice to biblical teaching which the theology was meant to summarize and systematize; in particular it inadequately expresses the biblical teaching on grace and on the Trinity. (It will become clear how closely interwoven these two matters were in Edwards' thinking.) In the *Treatise on Grace* he says 'If we suppose no more than used to be supposed about the Holy Ghost, the honour of the Holy Ghost in the work of redemption is not equal in any sense to the Father and the Son's; nor is there an equal part of the glory of this work belonging to Him. Merely to apply to us, or immediately to give or hand to us blessing purchased, after it is purchased, is subordinate to the other two Persons ... But according to what has now been supposed, there is an equality. To be the wonderful love of God, is as much as for the Father and the Son to exercise wonderful love; and to be the thing purchased, is as much as to be the price that purchases it. The price, and the thing bought with that price, answers each other in value; and to be the excellent benefit offered,

INTRODUCTION

is as much as to offer such an excellent benefit.' (p. 67–8. Cf. the
similar passage on pp. 123–4 of the *Essay*, and also *Observations*,
p. 88 'The Spirit was the inheritance that Christ, as God-man,
purchased for Himself and His Church'). The Holy Spirit is not
the agent of application, He is what is given to the Church.

This modification, which is clearly one *within* the Westminster
covenantal framework and not *of* it, is in the interests of securing
two important gains. Firstly, Edwards' aims to highlight the
immediacy and *uniqueness* of the gift of divine grace conveyed into
the soul. Each of these teachings is prominent throughout Edwards'
work; in 1734, when he was thirty-one, his sermon, 'A Divine
and Supernatural Light immediately imparted to the Soul, shown
to be both a Scriptural and Rational doctrine' was published. This
is a firm declaration of the truth that the Spirit of God 'acts in the
mind of a saint as an indwelling, vital principle . . . he unites himself with the mind of a saint, takes him for his temple, actuates
and influences him as a new supernatural principle of life and
action . . . Holiness is the proper nature of the Spirit of God.'[1] This
immediate divine light 'reveals no new doctrine, it suggests no
new proposition to the mind, it teaches no new thing of God, or
Christ, or another world, not taught in the Bible, but only gives
a due apprehension of those things that are taught in the word of
God.'

In his famous *Religious Affections* the negative consequences of
this stress were worked out in the light of the enthusiastic, antinomian excesses of the Great Awakening; a true work of God in
the soul is not to be identified with bodily or psychological dis-
turbances which could have a natural explanation, such as a readi-
ness to talk about religion, or the occurrence to the mind of texts
of scripture. A true work of grace consists in the Spirit of God
being 'given to the true saints to dwell in them, as his proper
lasting abode; and to influence their hearts, as a principle of new
nature, or as a divine supernatural spring of life and action'.[2]
Christian practice is the true sign of such a work, both to our-

[1] *Works*, vol. ii, p. 13.
[2] *Works*, vol. i, p. 265.

selves and to others. The point is further elaborated in *Distinguishing Marks of a Work of the Spirit of God* (1741) and in his sermon 'True Grace Distinguished from the Experience of Devils', published in 1752.

Further, this experience of divine grace is unique. Edwards makes this point by means of a distinction between common and special grace, or, equally often, between natural and supernatural experiences. The elaboration of this distinction is the main purpose of the *Treatise on Grace*. 'Special or saving grace . . . is not only different from common grace in degree, but entirely diverse in nature and kind.' (p. 25.) It follows that conversion (i.e. regeneration) must be instantaneous and 'it is impossible for men to convert themselves' (p. 36–7). The importance of this for Edwards' Calvinism is obvious; but what is just as important is the way in which it makes man immediately dependent on God. A man cannot keep God at a distance either by his autonomous, self-determining will (this is Edwards' argument in the *Freedom of the Will*), nor by endeavouring to prepare himself for grace. Such preparation, though a duty, can only 'increase and improve and new-model and direct qualities, principles, and perfections of nature that they have already' (*Treatise*, p. 37). 'Grace must be the immediate work of God, and properly a production of His almighty power on the soul.' (p. 38.) As Professor James Carse has recently put it:

> Once a person has supposed that he can put himself into the alcove of his soul without any real connection with what passes by on the outside, he takes his relationship with God out of history. Now there is no public act of God—no commandment, no moral government, no ecclesiastical institution—that can in the least influence our relationship to him if we do not want it to. Our business with God will be *where we like it* and *when we choose*.[1]

It was this 'distancing' of men from God that Edwards emphatically opposed.

So it is strictly inappropriate to speak of 'habits of grace'. 'All

[1] *Jonathan Edwards & The Visibility of God*, Scribner's. New York, 1967, p. 62.

succeeding acts of grace must be as immediately, and, to all intents and purposes, as much from the immediate acting of the Spirit of God on the soul, as the first.' (p. 74.) It is this point about the immediate dependence of man on God that is behind Edwards' famous imprecatory sermons which many have found so repellant. Their titles make this clear—'God glorified in Man's Dependence', 'Sinners in the hands of an angry God'. Whatever may be thought of the propriety of the language used in these sermons, it is clear that they are not the work of a ranter but were designed to impress the minds of his hearers with the truth about themselves as he saw it. This emphasis on immediate dependence was also an important factor in his opposition to the 'half-way' covenant of Solomon Stoddard which led to his dismissal from Northampton in 1750.

The fact that the tests of such a supernatural work of grace are ethical does not mean that in Edwards' view the supernatural is reduced to the ethical. He had no Kantian difficulties about knowing that God had revealed Himself in history and through Scripture, but he was confronted with an acute pastoral problem posed by the Great Awakening; how can a man know truly that God is at work in his life? Edwards' answer to this was unequivocal, 'gracious affections have their exercise and fruit in christian practice'. Christian practice is a sufficient test of Christian grace; but this does not mean that Christian practice is Christian grace.

Edwards' contrast between common and special grace is firmly tied by him to ethics in the following way: the natural man is dominated by self-love; the spiritual man loves 'being in general'. His views on ethics were propounded in *A Dissertation on the Nature of True Virtue*, posthumously published in 1765. There he argues that true virtue consists in love to being in general. 'True virtue most essentially consists in BENEVOLENCE TO BEING IN GENERAL. Or perhaps, to speak more accurately, it is that consent, propensity, and union of heart to being in general, which is immediately exercised in a general good will.'[1] It follows, Edwards argues, 'that true virtue must chiefly consist in LOVE

[1] *Works*, vol. i, p. 122.

To GOD, the Being of beings, infinitely the greatest and best'.[1]

This connection between grace and ethics is very clear in the *Treatise on Grace*. 'He that is once brought to see, or rather to taste, the superlative loveliness of the Divine Being, will need no more to make him long after the enjoyment of God, to make him rejoice in the happiness of God, and to desire that this supremely excellent Being may be pleased and glorified.' (p. 48) Thus by love to 'being in general' Edwards means a love that has God, the supreme and infinitive being, as its chief object and sufficient condition. 'Therefore he that has true virtue, consisting in benevolence to being in general, and in benevolence to *virtuous* being, must necessarily have a supreme love to God, both of benevolence and complacence.'[2] One important component of this love to God as Edwards shows both in the *Treatise* and in the *Affections* is love to God *for his own sake*. 'The main ground of true love to God is the excellency of His own nature, and not any benefit we have received, or hope to receive, by His goodness to us . . . love or affection to God, that has no other good than only some benefit received or hoped for from God, is not true love.' (p. 49) Compare this rather Kantian stance with the *Affections*, Part III, Section II; '*The first objective of gracious affections, is the transcendently excellent and amiable nature of divine things, as they are in themselves; and*

[1] *Works*, vol. i, p. 125.

[2] *Works*, vol. i, p. 125. A. V. G. Allen in *Jonathan Edwards*, p. 359 accuses Edwards of inconsistency at this point in an effort to show that the *Treatise on Grace* represents a later and better phase of Edwards' thought than that found in *Virtue*. He says that whereas in *Virtue* Edwards gave pride of place to love of benevolence as the primary ground of virtue, to which he subordinated love of complacence, this is reversed in the *Treatise*. This apparent turn-about is resolved by the consideration that in *Virtue* Edwards placed love to being in general (in which, he says virtue essentially consists) as prior to both love of benevolence and love of complacence. He argues in chapter 1 of *Virtue* that complacence and benevolence presuppose beauty otherwise 'that would be to suppose that the beauty of intelligent beings primarily consisted in love to beauty; or that their virtue first of all consists in their love to virtue. Which is an inconsistence, and going in a circle.' 'Therefore . . . the primary object of virtuous love is being, simply considered.' This Edwards calls 'absolute' or 'pure' benevolence. Pure benevolence necessarily brings about complacence, which in turn produces benevolence 'out of gratitude to him for his love to general existence'.

not any conceived relation they bear to self, or self interest.' Edwards'
argument here, as elsewhere in the *Affections* is that the natural man
is capable of loving God for selfish reasons, but not of loving God
as He is in himself. 'A natural principle of self-love may be the
foundation of great affections towards God and Christ, without
seeing anything of the beauty and glory of the divine nature.
There is a certain gratitude that is a mere natural thing.'[1]

It is often asserted that Edwards was a mystic,[2] and certainly
isolated phrases may give countenance to this view. But his general
position is clear. The imparted Spirit enlightens the mind with
regard to what Edwards calls 'divine things', the Biblical message
of salvation through Christ. 'There is a new understanding of the
excellent nature of God and his wonderful perfections, some new
view of Christ in his spiritual excellencies and fulness, or things
are opened to him in a new manner, whereby he now understands those divine and spiritual doctrines which once were foolishness unto him.'[3] This is not mysticism. The experience of divine
grace leads to the individual *judging* that such and such is the case.[4]
There is no claim to 'cosmic consciousness', and Edwards guards
himself against excess by making certain qualifications. (See e.g.
p. 109 of the *Essay*.) Edwards is reaffirming the classic Puritan
insistence on Word *and* Spirit.

And what about the relation between this imparting of grace
and justification by faith? A man trusts Christ as a result of the
imparting of divine life and light. Theologically, faith is the gift of
God's grace; psychologically, a man believes when the object of
belief is taken to be worthy of belief, and this happens, according
to Edwards, when a man is given a sense of the beauty of divine
things. Justification is by faith alone, but Edwards' teaching about
the implanting of divine life enables him to do justice to his belief
that the faith that justifies is never alone. This is one reason why

[1] *Works*, vol. i, p. 275.
[2] e.g. by G. P. Fisher, 'The Philosophy of Jonathan Edwards', in *Discussions on History and Theology*, New York 1880, pp. 227, 228.
[3] *Works*, vol. i, p. 282.
[4] See Conrad Cherry, *The Theology of Jonathan Edwards: A Reappraisal*, Garden City, New York 1966, p. 23.

he hesitates over labelling faith *the* condition of justification. Faith is not the necessary and sufficient condition for justification. 'If it be that with which, or which being supposed, a thing shall be, and without which, or it being denied, a thing shall not be, we in such a case call it a condition of that thing. But in this sense faith is not the only condition of salvation or justification; for there are many things that accompany and flow from faith, with which justification shall be, and without which it will not be, and therefore are found to be put in Scripture in conditional propositions with justification and salvation, in multitudes of places; such are love to God, and love to our brethren, forgiving men their trespasses, and many other good qualifications and acts.'[1] (See also the Appendix to *Observations*, p. 96).

So far we have sketched Edwards' views of grace as the communication of divine life and the connection of this with ethics. Edwards' trinitarian views form to a great extent the other side of this coin. It has already been seen that Edwards is unhappy merely to speak of the Holy Spirit as the *applier* of redemption on account of the fact that this does not do justice to the deity of the Holy Spirit. It is now time to develop this a little more fully.

The *excursus* on the Trinity in Chapter 3 of the *Treatise* is to be taken as an attempt by Edwards to understand the nature of grace more fully by showing what, according to Scripture is 'the nature of the Holy Spirit' (p. 56). Here he expounds his view that the Holy Spirit is best understood as the personal love of God the Father. It is in this sense that Edwards understands the Apostle John's assertion that God is love. The 'is' here is that of identity; that is, the love of which John speaks is not merely the result of the Spirit's work in the regenerate it *is* the Spirit. Hence his frequent reference to 'communication'. (Cf. the *Essay* at this point; 'God is love' shows 'Love to be essential and necessary to the deity so that his nature consists in it.' (p. 98; also p. 106–7).) Edwards further claims that it is since God's love is primarily to himself, that the love of the Father is the Spirit; and it is because the Holy Spirit is, in this incomprehensible manner, the personal love of God, that

[1] *Works*, vol. i, p. 623. 'Justification by Faith Alone.'

we never read in the Bible of the Son loving the Spirit, or of the love of the Holy Spirit to men, or of communion or fellowship with the Holy Spirit (*Treatise*, p. 62; *Essay*, p. 116).

The upshot of this is that each person of the Trinity is to be regarded as having an equal part in the work of redemption. 'There is an equal glory due to the Holy Ghost on this account, because He is the love of the Father and the Son, that flows out primarily towards God, and secondarily towards the elect that Christ came to save.' (*Treatise*, p. 66.) And hence it is that the New Testament speaks of grace as 'spiritual'; 'it is of the nature of the Spirit' (p. 68).[1]

Further, the insistence on the equality of the persons of the trinity and their co-operation in man's redemption makes any denial of Edwards' commitment to classic Reformed covenant theology extremely hard to credit. That Edwards abandond the covenant theology of his fathers, in spirit if not always in the letter, is the claim of Perry Miller in his important and influential study of Edwards,[2] and of P. Y. de Jong in *The Covenant Idea in New England Theology*.[3]

In order to estimate the force of these objections it will be necessary to make a few general remarks about covenant theology. Many Reformed theologians, Edwards included, make the distinction between the covenant of redemption, and the covenant of grace. The former refers to the trinitarian 'agreement' to redeem; the latter to the covenant relation between Christ and the church. Edwards puts it in the following way: 'It seems to me, there arises considerable confusion from not rightly distinguishing between the covenant that God made with Christ and with His church or believers in Him, and the covenant between Christ and His church, or between Christ and men. There is doubtless a difference

---

[1] The significance of Edwards' trinitarianism for his ethics has been discussed by Henry Stob, 'The Ethics of Jonathan Edwards' in *Faith and Philosophy*, ed. A. Plantinga, Grand Rapids 1964, pp. 111–37. See also R. A. Delattre, *Beauty and Sensibility in the Thought of Jonathan Edwards*, New Haven 1968.

[2] *Jonathan Edwards*, 1949. (Republished by Meridian Books, 1959. Page references are to this edition.)

[3] Grand Rapids 1945.

between the covenant that God makes with Christ and His people, considered as one, and the covenant of Christ and His people between themselves.' (*Observations*, Appendix, p. 94–5, also p. 96.)

It is clear to start with that Edwards was, in general terms, a 'covenant theologian'. Besides his bold trinitarianism already discussed there are two other important pieces of evidence to support this; certain external details of his life, and his explicit avowal of this doctrine in the *Observations*.

The external details are quite straightforward; writing in 1746 to his friend and former pupil, Joseph Bellamy, and referring to two standard exponents of covenant theology, Van Mastricht and Turretine, Edwards states: 'They are both excellent. Turretine is on polemical divinity; on the 5 points, and all other controversial points; and is much larger in these than Mastricht; and is better for one that desires only to be thoroughly versed in controversies. But take Mastricht for divinity in general doctrine Practice and Controversie; or as an universal system of divinity; and is much better than Turretine, or any other Book in the world, excepting the Bible, in my opinion.'[1] Elsewhere Edwards refers to 'the great Turretine'. Further, when Edwards was dismissed from his church at Northampton in 1750 he was approached by his Scottish friend and correspondent John Erskine, about the possibility of emigrating to Scotland. Edwards replied that there would be 'no difficulty' in subscribing to the substance of the Westminster Confession.[2]

Edwards' *Observations* support this. The chief point he makes is that the persons of the Trinity ought not to be understood in terms of their role in redemption, but *vice versa*: the headship of the Father in the Trinity is shown by his choice of the Son as the mediator of the Covenant and the redeemer of the church (p. 79). Again, God's determination to communicate Himself in the creation of the universe is prior to His determination to redeem. The natural equality of the members of the Trinity means that

---

[1] Letter to Joseph Bellamy, 15th January 1746, printed by F. B. Dexter, 'On the Manuscripts of Jonathan Edwards', in *Massachusetts Historical Society Proceedings*, Second Series, vol. xv, pp. 12–13, 1902.

[2] *Works*, vol. i, p. clxiii.

the subordination of the Son and the Holy Spirit must be *covenantal* not ontological in character. The Sonship of Christ is eternal (p. 91–2) and when redemption is complete the ontologica Ttrinity remains. There is no space to discuss the complex issues raised here but Edwards' commitment to covenant theology is clearly shown both by the orthodoxy of his views and the fact that he expounds them with his customary reverence, intellectual intensity and thoroughness.

But what about Edwards' commitment to the covenantal character of the relationship between God and His church? It is this that Miller questions, on the grounds of Edwards stress on the immediacy of the grace of God and the dependence of man on God, the very points brought out in this Introduction. Is Miller warranted in drawing the conclusion that he does? He makes two points about the popular presentation of covenant theology in Edwards' day, that 'At the moment of conversion . . . the saint is received into a compact with the divine, and thereafter depends for his security upon the fact that the transaction is on record' and that 'by conceiving of regeneration as the drawing up of a covenant, requiring assent on both sides, the clergy could, even while professing absolute predestination, offer to men rational inducements for their attempting to open negotiations'.[1] Supposing that these are historically accurate claims, it is clear that the first has an antinomian thrust, while the second is Pelagian and legalistic. Opposition to both of these does not entail denial of the convenantal character of the relationship between God and men.[2] What Edwards is doing is re-stating the *sovereignly gracious* character of the covenantal relationship, for which 'christian practice' is the

---

[1] Perry Miller, *Jonathan Edwards*, p. 30, also pp. 76–77.

[2] Miller's claim that in his sermon 'God glorified in Man's Dependence' Federal Theology is conspicuous by its utter absence (p. 30) is untrue. Several passages are explicitly 'covenantal' e.g. 'Jesus Christ is not only of God in his person, as he is the only-begotten Son of God, but he is from God, as we are concerned in him, and in his office of Mediator. He is the gift of God to us: God chose and anointed him, appointed him his work, and sent him into the world. And as it is God that *gives*, so it is God that *accepts* the Saviour.' *Works*, vol. ii, p. 3.

only firm ground of assurance. Any attempt to 'rationally induce' men to come to God, implies a Pelagian view of the will and is implicitly naturalistic; pastorally, it is counter-productive, for it imples that men have the power to, and hence could afford to postpone their turning to God; but they could not afford to think of postponement if they were 'in the hands' of God. Edwards' preaching was a reaffirmation of the gracious, holy character of God's convenantal dealings with men. And he was being quite consistent in asserting in public that 'the redeemed are in everything directly, immediately and entirely dependent on God for all their good' while elaborating in his private notebooks the orthodox distinction between the covenant of redemption and the covenant of grace.

P. Y. de Jong also judges that Edwards is guilty of departing from classic covenant theology. Though his allegiance to Calvinism is acknowledged yet de Jong argues that Edwards 'did perhaps more than anyone else toward preparing for the complete and final eradication of this idea (i.e the covenant) from New England religious life'. He is accused of 'Anabaptist individualistic piety'; in his hands the covenant idea became 'no more than an anthropological representation of God's dealings with men'.[1] The grounds for this charge are mainly three; his championing of revival, his doctrines of imputation and of the will, and his ecclesiology. But de Jong fails to show that Edwards' discriminating endorsement of revival is inconsistent with covenant theology. Edwards' teaching on imputation and the will are connected. If, as B. B. Warfield[2] and John Murray[3] have argued, Edwards taught the immediate imputation of Adam's sin to his posterity, it is hard to see how de Jong can fairly claim that Edwards denied Adam's federal headship and so depart from the 'organic conceptions so strongly embedded in the Calvinism of Scotland and the Netherlands'.[4]

[1] The Covenant Idea in New England Theology, pp. 150, 143.
[2] 'Edwards and the New England Theology', in Hastings, Encyclopaedia of Religion and Ethics, reprinted in Studies in Theology, New York 1932.
[3] The Imputation of Adam's Sin, Grand Rapids 1959, p. 54.
[4] op. cit., p. 150.

On ecclesiology it is true that Edwards made active faith a pre-requisite for attending communion, and tied regeneration and faith closely together. But do either of these positions entail a departure from covenant theology? It seems at times that Edwards is being faulted for what later New England theologians made of his position. B. B. Warfield's estimate that 'what he teaches is just the "standard" Calvinism in its completeness' is beyond serious dispute.

Space forbids more than a brief mention of two further points about Edwards' theology which these writings highlight. For all his reaffirmation of orthodoxy it is clear that he is not averse to theological development. (See for example his statement on the biblical teaching on the Trinity on p. 125–6 of the *Essay*.) But his view of development is determined by his view of faith and reason and the authority of Scripture. His theological method is to test such developments by the way they illuminate scripture and cohere with what it already clearly teaches. Secondly, he took very seriously the imagery of the Bible. This comes out clearly in the closing pages of the *Essay* where he argues that the sun in particular is a representation of the Trinity. As Miller has pointed out in his Introduction to Edwards' manuscript, *Images or Shadows of Divine Things*,[1] he regarded biblical language not as rhetorical embellishment, but as figures and types intended to convey *truth*. It is therefore no mere literary accident that, say, the colours of the rainbow are used to illustrate certain particular biblical truths. The imagery is appropriate because the natural order is a shadow of the spiritual. The expositor must therefore spiritualize on the basis of the lead that scripture gives in the matter, otherwise he will inevitably get in bondage to his own fancy.

III. PHILOSOPHICAL

Edwards' major philosophical work is of course *Freedom of the Will*, but the items reprinted here are not without interest from a philosophical standpoint. Three matters will be touched on briefly;

[1] New Haven 1948.

his indebtedness to Locke, his 'ontological proof'of the Trinity, and his general position on the question of faith and reason.

Locke.

Edwards self-confessed dependence on Locke is well known. But what is its exact extent? This is a large question[1] but the evidence of these items reprinted here is that Edwards used Locke where it suited him, rather than followed him uncritically. It is one of the oddities of the history of ideas that whereas many of Edwards' contemporaries in Britain found the seeds of deism in Locke[2], Edwards used him to buttress Calvinism

The most obvious influence of Locke occurs in Edwards' use of his terminology to enforce the supernatural character of divine grace. This is most evident of all in the *Affections* but it comes out also in the *Treatise* in what Edwards says about *meaning*. Expounding *I Corinthians* xi, 14 in light of his doctrine of the 'new sense' Edwards says of a man without divine grace 'He does not know what the talk of such things (viz. 'divine things') means; they are words without a meaning to him; he knows nothing of the matter any more than a blind man of colours' (p. 28).

This is the Lockean theory of meaning; words without ideas to match them are meaningless. The use of words is to be 'sensible marks of *ideas*, and the *ideas* they stand for are their proper and immediate signification'.[3] Hence someone who lacks the 'new sense of things' finds the language meaningless. He has no ideas for which the words used stand. In his chapter 'Of Faith and Reason, and their Distinct Provinces', Locke has an interesting section on 'new simple ideas' in which he asserts that a revelation of new simple ideas is necessarily incommunicable. Edwards never tackles the problems of communication between those possessing the new sense; they communicated, and that was sufficient. But

---

[1] I have discussed some aspects of it in an article 'John Locke and Jonathan Edwards: A reconsideration', in *Journal of the History of Philosophy*, vol. viii, no. 1, January 1969.

[2] See J. W. Yolton, *John Locke and the Way of Ideas*, London 1956.

[3] Locke, *Essay*, Book III, ch. 2. s. 1.

it is safe to say what he would reply—that God communicates new simple ideas not in the sense of giving new information which others cannot know but in the sense that he makes certain propositions *worthy to be believed*, and part of this change is moral. Thus the test of whether a man has this new sense or not is public—'christian practice'. Edwards' problem was less that of how men could communicate than that of preventing men from thinking that participation in the life and language of a religious community was a sufficient condition of divine grace. There was plenty of religious language in New England, but little Christian practice. That one could participate in the public religious language was not sufficient to show that one had true spiritual understanding. Love is the test of the reality of 'divine work' within a man.

This discussion raises many complex issues in the philosophy of mind and the philosophy of language which cannot be gone into here. The problems about the meaning of expressions that refer to one's private states, and how these are best analysed, are at the centre of modern discussion. However, it is fairly clear that Edwards is committed to an empiricist theory of meaning even though he has different views from Locke on the scope and limits of human knowledge. (See the discussion on 'faith and reason' below).

Consistently with his position on meaning Edwards follows Locke on definition. Locke had argued that 'the *names of simple ideas*, and those only, *are incapable of being defined*'.[1] The reason for this is that ideas are simple, uncompounded. Since a definition (in the sense in which Locke is using the word) is the definition of a word by another word or words there can be no definition of simple ideas. They have no features that can be picked out by a *definiens*. The meaning of simple ideas is 'to be *got* by those *impressions* objects themselves make in our minds, by the proper inlets appointed to each sort. If they are not received this way, all the *words* in the world, *made use of to explain or define any of their names, will never be able to produce in us the* idea *it stands for.*'[2]

Can the divine love which is communicated to the hearts of

[1] *Essay*, Book III, ch. iv. s. 7.
[2] *Essay*, Book III, ch. iv. s. 11.

God's people be defined? Edwards' answer to this is a firm negative. 'Things of this nature are not properly capable of a definition.
They are better felt than defined.' (*Treatise*, p. 47.) The new
simple idea is *sui generis*; any definition of it would be a natural-
izing of the supernatural character of the divine work in the soul.

The 'ontological proof' of the Trinity.

The ideas terminology that Edwards derived partly at least
from Locke, is carried over into the *Essay on the Trinity*. B. B.
Warfield calls it an attempt at an 'ontological proof'[1] of the
Trinity. Edwards argues as follows: if God has an idea of something absolutely perfect 'there is nothing in the pattern but what is
in the representation'. As, according to Edwards an idea of love is
an instance of love, so God's idea of Himself is Himself. 'Therefore
as God with perfect clearness, fullness and strength, understands
Himself, views His own essence (in which there is no distinction of
substance and act but which is wholly substance and wholly act)
that idea which God hath of Himself is absolutely Himself.' (p.
101.) This is an ingenious and bold argument, which might fairly
be called 'ontological'. To have an idea of x, where x is 'non-
material' is for x to exist. Hence God's idea of Himself, a most
perfect spirit, is Himself, i.e. is what the Bible calls the Word of
God. And the necessary affection that arises between God and His
Word is the Holy Spirit. 'This is the eternal and most perfect and
essential act of the Divine nature, wherein the Godhead acts in an
infinite degree and in the post perfect manner possible. The deity
becomes all act, the divine essence itself flows out and is as it were
breathed forth in love and joy. So that the Godhead therein stands
forth in yet another manner of subsistence, and there proceeds the
third Person in the Trinity, the Holy Spirit, viz. the deity in act,
for there is no other act but the act of the will.' (p. 106.)

The difficulty with this is clear. For one thing Edwards' premiss
that an idea of x where x is 'non-material', e.g. an emotion, is

---

[1] B. B. Warfield, 'The Biblical Doctrine of the Trinity', in *Biblical and
Theological Studies*, Philadelphia 1952, p. 26.

equivalent to an instance of x, is dubious. A person does not have to be in a fright to have an idea of fear. But disregarding this, what God's idea of Himself will be will not be another person of the Godhead but another God. If a perfect idea of x entails that x exists then Edwards has proved too much—not the second person of a trinity of persons but a second *theos*. His argument is implicitly tri-theistic. It is clear however from the *Essay* that he does not regard this as a convincing proof. He considers objections, particularly that his thesis would deny personality to the Holy Ghost (p. 118), and fully allows the limitations of his case. 'But I don't pretend fully to explain how these things are and I am sensible a hundred other objections may be made and puzzling doubts and questions raised that I can't solve. I am far from pretending to explaining the Trinity so as to render it no longer a mystery. I think it to be the highest and deepest of all divine mysteries still, notwithstanding anything I have said or conceived about it. I don't intend to explain the Trinity.'[1] (p. 119–20.) Edwards was a metaphysician, but he was no rationalist. The mysteries of revelation were to be mysteries still.

His motive was not rationalistic; rather he wanted to say a little more than had been said before within the limits of the biblical data and thereby to make things as 'easy and intelligible' as possible. His argument was less an attempt at a formal proof of the Trinity than a model in terms of which more justice could be done to the biblical record than previously.

Faith and Reason.

Edwards lived in the Age of Reason, and he did not despise the use of the intellect. Yet reasoning was to be subordinated to the authority of Scripture, which Edwards took with absolute seriousness, and which has made him into such a tragic figure

---

[1] Compare 'Rabbi' Duncan, 'The Trinity is my highest Theologoumenon. I reach it, and find in it the supreme harmony of revealed things. But it is equally irrational and irreverent to speculate on the nexus between the Persons. This is not revealed, and I think it is not revealable.' *Colloquia Peripatetica*, 5th edn., Edinburgh 1879, p. 165.

to later liberal commentators. Reason was to be used not so much to provide a rational foundation to Christian belief (Edwards says remarkably little about the 'theistic proofs') as to undergird biblical doctrine where possible (as in the *Freedom of the Will* where he provided a metaphysical refutation of Arminianism by showing the incoherence of the notion of the self-determining power of the will), and to enable faith to seek understanding (as in the *Essay*).[1]

Though, as has been shown, he had debts to Locke, the latter's way of relating faith to reason was not one of them. On Locke's view, revelation is natural reason enlarged by a new set of disclosures about past, present and future, communicated by God, e.g. 'that part of the angels rebelled against God and thereby lost their first happy state, and that the dead shall rise and live again'.[2] This information from God is to be believed; this is the province of faith, while reason vouches the truth of the revelation by accepting certain testimonies and proofs that accompany the revelation and that show it to be from God. Revelation covers those things that men are not in the best position to know, but even these must be consistent with the *'clear and self-evident dictates of reason'*.[3] Any truth from God will be accompanied 'by some marks which reason cannot be mistaken in'. But as Locke does not say what 'truths above reason' are, nor provide any criterion for distinguishing '*x* comes from God' from '*x* does not come from God' this position is hardly a stable or satisfactory one.

For Edwards on the other hand the Bible was God's revelation to which the one possessed of the new sense of divine things would willingly submit himself. But this does not entail that a man's reason is inert, though it does close the door to any ratonalistic repudiation or reduction of Scripture. Reason's function is to be the elucidator of and apologete for the divine mysteries. Edwards uses 'reason' in two senses; in a strict sense, as logical argument, and in

---

[1] For a general statement of the relationship between reason and revelation see *Miscellaneous Observations on Important Theological Subjects*, ch. 7, in *Works*, vol. ii, pp. 479ff.

[2] *Essay*, Book IV, ch. xviii. s. 7.

[3] *Essay*, Book IV, ch. xviii. s. 10.

his work he continually exposes the logical incoherences of critics of Protestant orthodoxy like Whitby and Chubb (in *Freedom of the Will*) and Taylor of Norwich (in *Original Sin*). And he uses arguments to construct models to elucidate mysteries (as in the *Essay*) or to propound solutions to difficulties (as in *Original Sin*, when by a metaphysical argument about personal identity he tries to show that the whole of Adam's posterity was identical with Adam when he fell, and hence was culpable). But he was always ready, as has been shown, to acknowledge the limits of such speculations. Secondly, he uses 'reason' in a more informal sense, as when, in the *Treatise*, he writes that religion that has no true regard for God is 'unreasonable'.

TREATISE ON GRACE

I

SUCH phrases as common grace, and special or saving grace, may be understood as signifying either diverse kinds of influence of God's Spirit on the hearts of men, or diverse fruits and effects of that influence. The Spirit of God is supposed sometimes to have some influence upon the minds of men that are not true Christians, and [it is supposed] that those dispositions, frames, and exercises of their minds that are of a good tendency, but are common to them with the saints, are in some respect owing to some influence or assistance of God's Spirit. But as there are some things in the hearts of true Christians that are peculiar to them, and that are more excellent than any thing that is to be found in others, so it is supposed that there is an operation of the Spirit of God different, and that the value which distinguishes them is owing to a higher influence and assistance than the virtues of others. So that sometimes the phrase, *common grace*, is used to signify that kind of action or influence of the Spirit of God, to which are owing those religious or moral attainments that are common to both saints and sinners, and so signifies as much as common assistance; and sometimes those moral or religious attainments themselves that are the fruits of this assistance, are intended. So likewise the phrase, *special* or *saving* grace, is sometimes used to signify that peculiar kind or degree of operation or influence of God's Spirit, whence saving actions and attainments do arise in the godly, or, which is the same thing, special and saving assistance; or else to signify that distinguishing saving virtue itself, which is the fruit of this assistance. These phrases are more frequently understood in the latter sense, viz., nor for common and special assistance, but for common and special, or saving virtue, which is the fruit of that assistance, and so I would be understood by these phrases in this discourse.

And that special or saving grace in this sense is not only different from common grace in degree, but entirely diverse in nature and kind, and that natural men not only have not a sufficient degree of virtue to be saints, but that they have no degree of that grace that is in godly men, is what I have now to shew.

1. *This is evident by what Christ says in* John iii. 6, where Christ, speaking of regeneration, says—" That which is born of the flesh is flesh, and that which is born of the Spirit is spirit." Now, whatever Christ intends by the terms flesh and spirit in the words, yet this much is manifested and undeniable, that Christ here intends to shew Nicodemus the necessity of a new birth, or another birth than his natural birth, and that, from this argument, that a man that has been the subject only of the first birth, has nothing of that in his heart which he must have in order to enter into the kingdom. He has nothing at all of that which Christ calls spirit, whatever that be. All that a man [has] that has been the subject only of a natural birth don't go beyond that which Christ calls flesh, for however it may be refined and exalted, yet it cannot be raised above flesh. 'Tis plain, that by flesh and spirit, Christ here intends two things entirely different in nature, which cannot be one from the other. A man cannot have anything of a nature superior to flesh that is not born again, and therefore we must be " born again." That by flesh and spirit are intended certain moral principles, natures, or qualities, entirely different and opposite in their nature one to another, is manifest from other texts, as particularly: Gal. v. 17—" For the flesh lusteth against the spirit, and the spirit against the flesh: and they are contrary the one to the other; so that ye cannot do the things which ye would"; Ver. 19, " Now the works of the flesh are manifest, which are these; Adultery, fornication," etc. Ver. 22—" But the fruit of the Spirit is love, joy, peace," etc.; and by Gal. vi. 8—" For he that soweth to the flesh shall of the flesh reap corruption: but he that soweth to the Spirit shall of the Spirit reap life everlasting." Rom. viii. 6–9—" For to be carnally minded is death, but to be spiritually minded is life and peace" etc. 1 Cor. iii. 1—" And I, brethren, could not speak

unto you as unto spiritual, but as unto carnal, even as unto babes in Christ." So that it is manifest by this, that men that have been the subjects only of the first birth, have no degree of that moral principle or quality that those that are new born have, whereby they have a title to the kingdom of heaven. This principle or quality comes out then no otherwise than by birth, and the birth that it must come by is not, cannot be, the first birth, but it must be a new birth. If men that have no title to the kingdom of heaven, could have something of the Spirit, as well as flesh, then Christ's argument would be false. It is plain, by Christ's reasoning, that those that are not in a state of salvation, cannot have these two opposite principles in their hearts together, some flesh and some spirit, lusting one against the other as the godly have, but that they have flesh only.

2. *That the only principle in those that are savingly converted, whence gracious acts flow, which in the language of Scripture is called the Spirit, and set in opposition to the flesh, is that which others not only have not a sufficient degree of, but have nothing at all of,* is further manifest, *because the Scripture asserts both negatively, that those that have not the Spirit are not Christ's.* Rom. viii. 9—" But ye are not in the flesh but in the Spirit, if so be that the Spirit of God dwell in you. Now if any man have not the Spirit of Christ, he is none of his"; *and also* [positively] *that those that have the Spirit are His.* 1 John iii. 24—" Hereby we know that he abideth in us by the Spirit which he hath given us." And our having the Spirit of God dwelling in our hearts is mentioned as a certain sign that persons are entitled to heaven, and is called the earnest of the future inheritance, (2 Cor. i. 22, and v. 5, Eph. i. 14); which it would not be if others that had no title to the inheritance might have some of it dwelling in them.

Yea, that those that are not true saints have nothing of the Spirit, no part nor portion of it, is still more evident, because not only a having any particular motion of the Spirit, but a being *of the Spirit* is given as a sure sign of being in Christ. 1 John iv. 13— " Hereby know we that we dwell in him, and he in us, because he hath given us *of his Spirit.*" If those that are not true saints have any degree of that spiritual principle, then though they have not so much, yet they have *of it*, and so that would be no sign that a person is in Christ. If those that have not a saving interest in Christ have nothing of the Spirit, then they have nothing; no degree of those graces that are the fruits of the Spirit, mentioned in Gal. v. 22—" But the fruit of the Spirit is love, joy, peace, longsuffering, gentleness, goodness, faith, meekness, temperance." Those fruits are here mentioned with that very design, that we may know whether we have the Spirit or no.

3. *Those that are not true saints, and in a state of salvation, not only have not so much of that holy nature and Divine principle that is in the hearts of the saints, but they do not partake of it,* because a being " *partakers of the divine nature* " is spoken of as the peculiar privilege of true saints, (2 Pet. i. 4.) It is evident that it is the true saints that the apostle is there speaking of. The words in this verse with the foregoing are these: " According as his divine power hath given unto us all things that pertain unto life and godliness, through the knowledge of him that hath called us to glory and virtue: whereby are given to us exceeding great and precious promises: that by these ye might be partakers of the divine nature, having escaped the corruption that is in the world through lust." The " divine nature " and " lust " are evidently here spoken of as two opposite principles in man. Those that are in the world, and that are the men of the world, have only the latter principle; but to be partakers of the Divine nature is spoken of as peculiar to them that are distinguished and separated from the world, by the free and sovereign grace of God giving them all things that pertain to life and godliness, giving the knowledge of Him and calling them to glory and virtue, and giving them the exceeding great and precious promises of the gospel, and that have escaped the corruption of the world of wicked men. And a being partakers of the Divine nature is spoken of, not only as peculiar to the saints, but as one of the highest privileges of the saints.

4. *That those that have not a saving interest in Christ have no degree of that relish and sense of spiritual things or things of the Spirit, of their Divine truth and excellency, which a true saint has, is evident by* 1 Cor. ii. 14—" The natural man receiveth not the things of the

Spirit of God: for they are foolishness unto him: neither can he know them, because they are spiritually discerned." A natural man is here set in opposition to a spiritual one, or one that has the Spirit, as appears by the foregoing and following verses. Such we have shewn already the Scripture declares all true saints to be, and no other. Therefore by natural men are meant those that have not the Spirit of Christ and are none of His, and are the subjects of no other than the natural birth. But here we are plainly taught that a natural man is perfectly destitute of any sense, perception, or discerning of those things of the Spirit. [We are taught that] by the words " he neither does nor can know them, or discern them"; so far from this they are " foolishness unto him"; he is a perfect stranger, so that he does not know what the talk of such things means; they are words without a meaning to him; he knows nothing of the matter any more than a blind man of colours.

Hence it will follow, that the sense of things of religion that a natural man has, is not only not to the same degree, but nothing of the same nature with that which a true saint has. And besides, if a natural person has the fruit of the Spirit, which is of the same kind with what a spiritual person has, then he experiences within himself the things of the Spirit of God; and how then can he be said to be such a stranger to them, and have no perception or discerning of them?

The reason why natural men have no knowledge of spiritual things is, because they have nothing of the Spirit of God dwelling in them. This is evident by the context: for there we are told that it is by the Spirit that these things are taught, (verses 10-12); godly persons in the next verse are called spiritual, because they have the Spirit dwelling in them. Hereby the sense again is confirmed, for natural men are in no degree spiritual; they have only nature and no Spirit. If they had anything of the Spirit, though not in so great a degree as the godly, yet they would be taught spiritual things, or things of the Spirit, in proportion to the measure of the Spirit that they had. The Spirit that searcheth all things would teach them in some measure. There would not be so great a difference that the one could perceive nothing of them, and that they should be foolishness to them, while to the other they appear divinely and remarkably wise and excellent, as they are spoken of in the context, (verses 6-9), and as such the apostle spoke here of discerning them.

The reason why natural men have no knowledge or perception of spiritual things is, because they have none of the anointing spoken of, (1 John ii. 27): " The anointing which ye have received of him, abideth in you, and you need not that any man teach you." This anointing is evidently spoken of here, as a thing peculiar to true saints. Ungodly men never had any degree of that holy oil poured upon them, and therefore have no discerning of spiritual things. Therefore none of that sense that natural men have of things of religion, is of the same nature with what the godly have. But to these they are totally blind. Therefore in conversion the eyes of the blind are opened. The world is wholly unacquainted with the Spirit of God, as appears by John xiv. 17, where we read about " the Spirit of truth whom the world cannot receive, because it knoweth him not."

5. *Those that go for those in religion that are not true saints and in a state of salvation have no charity, as is plainly implied in the beginning of the XIIIth chapter of the 1st Epistle to the Corinthians.* Therefore they have no degree of that kind of grace, disposition, or affection that is so called. So Christ elsewhere reproves the Pharisees, those high pretenders to religion among the Jews, that they had not the love of God in them, (John v. 42).

6. *That those that are not true saints have no degree of that grace that the saints have is evident, because they have no communion or fellowship with Christ.* If those that are not true saints partake of any of that Spirit, those holy inclinations and affections, and gracious acts of soul that the godly have from the indwelling of the Spirit of Christ, then they would have communion with Christ. The communion of saints with Christ does certainly very much consist in that receiving of His fulness and partaking of His grace spoken of, John i. 16—" Of his fulness have all we received, and grace for grace"; and in partaking of that Spirit which God gives not by measure unto Him. Partaking of Christ's holiness and grace, His

nature, inclinations, tendencies, love, and desires, comforts and delights, must be to have communion with Christ. Yea, a believer's communion *with* the Father and the Son does mainly consist in his partaking of the Holy Ghost, as appears by 2 Cor. xiii. 14—"The grace of the Lord Jesus Christ, and the love of God, and the *communion* of the Holy Ghost."

But that unbelievers have no fellowship or communion with Christ appears (1.) because they are not united to Christ. They are not in Christ. For the Scripture is very plain and evident in this, that those that are in Christ are actually in a state of salvation, and are justified, sanctified, accepted of Christ, and shall be saved. Phil. iii. 8, 9—"Yea doubtless, and I count all things but loss for the excellency of the knowledge of Christ Jesus my Lord: for whom I have suffered the loss of all things, and do count them but dung, that I may win Christ, and be found *in him*." 2 Cor. v. 17—"If any man be *in Christ*, he is a new creature: old things are passed away; behold, all things are become new." 1 John ii. 5— "But whoso keepeth his word, in him verily is the love of God perfected: hereby know we that we are *in him*"; and iii. 24—"He that keepeth His commandments dwelleth in him, and he in him. And hereby we know that he abideth in us, by the Spirit which he hath given us." But those that are not in Christ, and are not united to Him, can have no degree of communion with Him. For there is no communion without union. The members can have no communion with the head or participation of its life and health unless they are united to it. The branch must be united with the vine, otherwise there can be no communication from the vine to it, nor any partaking of any degree of its sap, or life, or influence. So without the union of the wife to the husband, she can have no communion in his goods. (2.) The Scripture does more directly teach that it is only true saints that have communion with Christ, as particularly this is most evidently spoken of as what belongs to the saints, and to them only, in 1 John i. 3, together with verses 6, 7—"That which we have seen and heard declare we unto you, that ye also may have fellowship with us: and truly our fellowship is with the Father, and with his Son Jesus Christ."

Ver. 6—" If we say that we have fellowship with Him, and walk
in darkness, we lie, and do not the truth: but if we walk in the
light, as he is in the light, we have fellowship one with another,
and the blood of Jesus Christ his Son cleanseth us from all sin."
Also in I Cor. i. 9—" God is faithful, by whom ye were called
unto the fellowship of his Son Christ Jesus our Lord."

7. *The Scripture speaks of the actual being of a truly holy and gracious
principle in the heart, as inconsistent with a man's being a sinner or a
wicked man.* I John iii. 9—"Whosoever is born of God doth not
commit sin; for his seed remaineth in him: and he cannot sin,
because he is born of God." Here it is needless to dispute what is
intended by this seed, whether it be a principle of true virtue and
a holy nature in the soul, or whether it be the word of God as the
cause of that virtue. For let us understand it in either sense, it
comes to much the same thing in the present argument; for if by
the seed is meant the word of God, yet when it is spoken of as
abiding in him that is born again, it must be intended, with respect
to its effect, as a holy principle in his heart: for the word of God
does not abide in one that is born again more than another, any
other way than in its effect. The word of God abides in the heart
of a regenerate person as a holy seed, a Divine principle there,
though it may be but as a seed, a small thing. The seed is a very
small part of the plant, and is its first principle. It may be in the
heart as a grain of mustard-seed, may be hid, and seem to be in
great measure buried in the earth. But yet it is inconsistent with
wickedness. The smallest degrees and first principles of a Divine
and holy nature and disposition are inconsistent with a state of sin;
whence it is said "he cannot sin." There is no need here of a
critical inquiry into the import of that expression; for doubtless so
much at least is implied through this, " his seed being in him," as
is inconsistent with his being a sinner or a wicked man. So that
this heavenly plant of true holiness cannot be in the heart of a
sinner, no, not so much as in its first principle.

8. *This is confirmed by the things that conversion is represented by in
the Scriptures, particularly its being represented as a work of creation.*
When God creates He does not merely establish and perfect the

things which were made before, but makes wholly and immediately something entirely new, either out of nothing, or out of that which was perfectly void of any such nature, as when He made man of the dust of the earth. " The things that are seen are not made of things that do appear." Saving grace in man is said to be the new man or a new creature, and corrupt nature the old man. If that nature that is in the heart of a godly man be not different in its nature and kind from all that went before, then the man might possibly have had the same things a year before, and from time to time from the beginning of his life, but only not quite to the same degree. And how then is grace in him, the new man or the new creature?

Again, conversion is often compared to a resurrection. Wicked men are said to be dead, but when they are converted they are represented as being by God's mighty and effectual power raised from the dead. Now there is no medium between being dead and alive. He that is dead has no degree of life; he that has the least degree of life in him is alive. When a man is raised from the dead, life is not only in a greater degree, but it is all new.

The same is manifest by conversion being represented as a new birth or as regeneration. Generation is not only perfecting what is old, but 'tis a begetting from the new. The nature and life that is then received has then its beginning: it receives its first principles.

Again, conversion in Scripture is represented as an opening of the eyes of the blind. In such a work those have light given them that were totally destitute of it before. So in conversion, stones are said to be raised up children to Abraham: while stones they are altogether destitute of all those qualities that afterwards render them the living children of Abraham, and not only had them not in so great a degree. Agreeably to this, conversion is said to be a taking away a heart of stone and a giving a heart of flesh. The man while unconverted has a heart of stone which has no degree of that life and sense that the heart of flesh has, because it yet remains a stone, than which nothing is further from life and sense.

Inference I.—From what has been said, I would observe *that it must needs be that conversion is wrought at once.* That knowledge, that reformation and conviction that is preparatory to conversion may be gradual, and the work of grace after conversion may be gradually carried on, yet that work of grace upon the soul whereby a person is brought out of a state of total corruption and depravity into a state of grace, to an interest in Christ, and to be actually a child of God, is in a moment.

It must needs be the consequence; for if that grace or virtue that a person has when he is brought into a state of grace be entirely different in nature and kind from all that went before, then it will follow that the last instant before a person is actually a child of God and in a state of grace, a person has not the least degree of any real goodness, and of that true virtue that is in a child of God.

Those things by which conversion is represented in Scripture hold forth the same thing. In creation something is brought out of nothing in an instant. God speaks and it is done, He commands and it stands fast. When the dead are raised, it is done in a moment. Thus when Christ called Lazarus out of his grave, it was not a gradual work. He said, "Lazarus, come forth," and there went life with the call. He heard His voice and lived. So Christ, John v. 25—"Verily, verily, I say unto you, The hour is coming, and now is, when the dead shall hear the voice of the Son of God: and they that hear shall live,"—which words must be understood of the work of conversion. In creation, being is called out of nothing and instantly obeys the call, and in the resurrection the dead are called into life: as soon as the call is given the dead obey.

By reason of this instantaneousness of the work of conversion, one of the names under which conversion is frequently spoken of in Scripture, is *calling:* Rom. viii. 28–30—"And we know that all things work together for good to them that love God, to them who are the called according to his purpose. For whom he did foreknow, he also did predestinate to be conformed to the image of his Son, that he might be the firstborn among many brethren. Moreover whom he did predestinate, them he also called; and whom he called, them he also justified; and whom he justified, them he also glorified." Acts ii. 37–39—"Now when they heard this, they were pricked in their heart, and said unto Peter and to the rest of the apostles, Men and brethren, what shall we do? Then Peter said unto them, Repent, and be baptized every one of you in the name of Jesus Christ for the remission of sins, and ye shall receive the gift of the Holy Ghost. For the promise is unto you, and to your children, and to all that are afar off, even as many as the Lord our God shall call." Heb. ix. 15, (last clause)—" That they which are called might receive the promise of eternal inheritance." 1 Thess. v. 23, 24—" And the very God of peace sanctify you wholly. . . . Faithful is he that calleth you, who also will do it." Nothing else can be meant in those places by calling than what Christ does in a sinner's saving conversion. By which it seems evident that it is done at once and not gradually; whereby Christ, through His great power, does but speak the powerful word and it is done, He does but call and the heart of the sinner immediately comes. It seems to be symbolised by Christ's calling His disciples, and their immediately following Him. So when He called Peter, Andrew, James, and John, they were minding other things; but at His call they immediately left all and followed Him. Matt. iv. 18–22—Peter and Andrew were casting a net into the sea, and Christ says to them as He passed by, Follow me; and it is said, they straightway left their nets and followed Him. So James and John were in the ship with Zebedee their father mending their nets, and He called them, and immediately they left the ship and their father and followed Him. So when Matthew was called: Matt. ix. 9—" And as Jesus passed forth from thence, he saw a man, named Matthew, sitting at the receipt of custom: and he saith unto him, Follow me. And he arose and followed him." Now whether they were then converted or not, yet doubtless Christ in thus calling His first disciples to a visible following of Him, represents to us the manner in which He would call men to be truly His disciples and spiritually to follow Him in all ages. There is something immediately and instantaneously put into their hearts at that call that they had nothing of before, that effectually disposes them to follow.

It is very manifest that almost all the miracles of Christ that He wrought when on earth were types of His great work of converting sinners, and the manner of His working those miracles holds forth the instantaneousness of the work of conversion. Thus when He healed the leper, which represented His healing us of our spiritual leprosy, He put forth His hand and touched him, and said, " I will; be thou clean." And immediately his leprosy was cleansed. Matt. viii. 3; Mark i. 42; Luke v. 13. And so, in opening the eyes of the blind, which represents His opening the eyes of our blind souls, (Matt. xx. 30, etc.). He touched their eyes, and immediately their eyes received sight, and they followed Him. So Mark x. 52; Luke xviii. 43. So when He healed the sick, which represents His healing our spiritual diseases, or conversion, it was done at once. Thus when He healed Simon's wife's mother, (Mark i. 31), He took her by the hand and lifted her up; and immediately the fever left her, and she ministered unto them. So when the woman which had the issue of blood touched the hem of Christ's garment, immediately the issue of blood stanched, (Luke viii. 44). So the woman that was bowed together with the spirit of infirmity, when Christ laid His hands upon her, immediately she was made straight, and glorified God, (Luke xiii. 12, 13); which represents that action on the soul whereby He gives an upright heart, and sets the soul at liberty from its bondage to glorify Him. So the man at the pool of Bethesda, when Christ bade him rise, take up his bed and walk, (he) was immediately made whole, (John v. 8, 9). After the same manner Christ cast out devils, which represents His dispossessing the devil of our souls in conversion; and so He settled the winds and waves, representing His subduing, in conversion, the heart of the wicked, which is like the troubled sea, when it cannot rest; and so He raised the dead, which represented His raising dead souls.

The same is confirmed by those things which conversion is compared to in Scripture. It is often compared to a resurrection. Natural men (as was said before) are said to be dead, and to be raised when they are converted by God's mighy effectual power from the dead. Now, there is no medium between being dead and alive; he that is dead has no degree of life in him, he that has the least degree of life in him is alive. When a man is raised from the dead, life is not only in a greater degree in him than it was before, but it is all new. The work of conversion seems to be compared to a raising the dead to life, in this very thing, even its instantaneousness, or its being done, as it were, at a word's speaking. As in John v. 25, (before quoted)—" Verily, verily, I say unto you, the hour is coming, and now is, when the dead shall hear the voice of the Son of God: and they that hear shall live." He speaks here of a work of conversion, as appears by the preceding verse; and by the words themselves, which speak of the time of this raising the dead, not only as to come hereafter, but as what was already come. This shews conversion to be an immediate instantaneous work, like to the change made on Lazarus when Christ called him from the grave: there went life with the call, and Lazarus was immediately alive. Immediately before the call sinners are dead or wholly destitute of life, as appears by the expression, " *The dead* shall hear the voice," and immediately after the call they are alive; yea, there goes life with the word, as is evident, not only because it is said they shall live, but also because it is said, they shall hear His voice. The first moment they have any life is the moment when Christ calls, and as soon as they are called, which further appears by what was observed before, even that a being called and converted are spoken of in Scripture as the same thing.

The same is confirmed (as observed before) from conversion being compared to a work of creation, which is a work wherein something is made either out of nothing, or out of that having no degree of the same kind of qualities and principles, as when God made man of the dust of the earth. Thus it is said, "If any man be in Christ he is a new creature"; which obviously implies that he is an exceeding diverse kind of creature from what he was before he was in Christ, that the principle or qualities that he has by which he is a Christian, are entirely new, and what there was nothing of, before he was in Christ.

Inference 2. Hence we may learn that *it is impossible for men to convert themselves* by their own strength and industry, with only a concurring assistance helping in the exercise of their natural abilities and principles of the soul, and securing their improvement. For what is gained after this manner is a gradual acquisition, and not something instantaneously begotten, and of an entirely different nature, and wholly of a separate kind, from all that was in the nature of the person the moment before. All that men can do by their own strength and industry is only gradually to increase and improve and new-model and direct qualities, principles, and perfections of nature that they have already. And that is evident, because a man in the exercise and improvement of the strength and principles of his own nature has nothing but the qualities, powers, and perfections that are already in his nature to work with, and nothing but them to work upon; and therefore 'tis impossible that by this only, anything further should be brought to pass, than only a new modification of what is already in the nature of the soul. That which is only by an improvement of natural qualities, principles, and perfections—let these things be improved never so much and never so industriously, and never so long, they'll still be no more than an improvement of those natural qualities, principles, and perfections; and therefore not anything of an essentially distinct and superior nature and kind.

'Tis impossible (as Dr Clarke observes) " that any effect should have any perfection that was not in the cause: for if it had, then that perfection would be caused by nothing."[1] 'Tis therefore utterly impossible that men's natural perfections and qualities in that exercise, and however assisted in that exercise, should produce in the soul a principle or perfection of a nature entirely different from all of them, or any manner of improvement or modification of them.

The qualities and principles of natural bodies, such as figure or motion, can never produce anything beyond themselves. If infinite comprehensions and divisions be eternally made, the things must still be eternally the same, and all their possible effects can

[1] Samuel Clarke (1675-1729) the famous eighteenth century theologian. –H.

never be anything but repetitions of the same. Nothing can be produced by only those qualities of figure and motion, beyond figure and motion: and so nothing can be produced in the soul by only its internal principles, beyond these principles or qualities, or new improvements and modifications of them. And if we suppose a concurring assistance to enable to a more full and perfect exercise of those natural principles and qualities, unless the assistance or influence actually produces something beyond the exercise of internal principle: still, it is the same thing. Nothing will be produced but only an improvement and new modification of those principles that are exercised. Therefore it follows that saving grace in the heart, can't be produced in man by mere exercise of what perfections he has in him already, though never so much assisted by moral suasion, and never so much assisted in the exercise of his natural principles, unless there be something more than all this, viz., an immediate infusion or operation of the Divine Being upon the soul. Grace must be the immediate work of God, and properly a production of His almighty power on the soul.

II

SHEWING WHEREIN ALL SAVING GRACE DOES SUMMARILY CONSIST

THE next thing that arises for consideration is, What is the nature of this Divine principle in the soul that is so entirely diverse from all that is naturally in the soul? Here I would observe,—

1. *That that saving grace that is in the hearts of the saints, that within them [which is] above nature, and entirely distinguishes 'em from all unconverted men, is radically but one—i.e., however various its exercises are, yet it is but one in its root; 'tis one individual principle in the heart.*

'Tis common for us to speak of various graces of the Spirit of God as though they were so many different principles of holiness, and to call them by distinct names as such,—repentance, humility, resignation, thankfulness, etc. But we err if we imagine that

39

these in their first source and root in the heart are properly distinct principles. They all come from the same fountain, and are, indeed, the various exertions and conditions of the same thing; only different denominations according to the various occasions, objects, and manners, attendants and circumstances of its exercise. There is some one holy principle in the heart that is the essence and sum of all grace, the root and source of all holy acts of every kind, and the fountain of every good stream, into which all Christian virtues may ultimately be resolved, and in which all duty and [all] holiness is fulfilled.

Thus the Scripture represents it. Grace in the soul is one fountain of water of life, (John iv. 14), and not various distinct fountains. So God, in the work of regeneration, implants one heavenly seed in the soul, and not various different seeds. 1 John iii. 9—" Whosoever is born of God doth not commit sin; for his *seed* remaineth in him." . . . The day [that] has arisen on the soul is but one. The oil in the vessel is simple and pure, conferred by one holy anointing. All is "wrought" by one individual work of the Spirit of God. And thus it is there is a consentanation of graces. Not only is one grace in some way allied to another, and so tends to help and promote one another, but one is really implied in the other. The nature of one involves the nature of another. And the great reason of it is, that all graces have one common essence, the original principle of all, and is but one. Strip the various parts of the Christian soul of their circumstances, concomitants, appendages, means, and occasions, and consider that which is, as it were, their *soul* and essence, and all apears to be the same. [I observe]

2. That principle in the soul of the saints, which is the grand Christian virtue, and which is the soul and essence and summary comprehension of all grace, *is a principle of Divine love.* This is evident,

(1.) *Because we are abundantly taught in the Scripture that Divine love is the sum of all duty;* and that all that God requires of us is fulfilled in it,—*i.e.*, That love is the sum of all duty of the heart, and its exercises and fruits the sum of all [the] duty of life. But if the duty of the heart, or all due dispositions of the hearts, are all summed up in love, then undoubtedly all grace may be summed up in LOVE.

The Scripture teaches us that all our duty is summed up in love; or, which is the same thing, that 'tis the sum of all that is required in the Law; and that, whether we take the Law as signifying the Ten Commandments, or the whole written Word of God. So, when by the Law is meant the Ten Commandments: Rom. xiii. 8—" Owe no man any thing, but to love one another: for he that loveth another hath fulfilled the law"; and, therefore, several of these commandments are there rehearsed. And again, in ver. 10, " Love is the fulfilling of the law." And unless love was the sum of what the law required, the law could not be fulfilled in love. A law is not fulfilled but by obedience to the sum of what it contains. So the same apostle again: 1 Tim. i. 5—"Now the end of the commandment is charity " [love].

If we take the law in a yet more extensive sense for the whole written Word of God, the Scripture still teaches us that love is the sum of what is required in it. [Thus] Matt. xxii. 40. There Christ teaches us that on these two precepts of loving God and our neighbour hang all the Law and the Prophets,—that is, all the written Word of God. So that what was called the Law and the Prophets was the whole written Word of God that was then extant. The Scripture teaches this of each table of the law in particular.

Thus, the lawyer that we read of in the Xth chapter of Luke, vv. 25–28, mentions the love of God and our neighbour as the sum of the two tables of the law; and Christ approves of what he says. When he stood up and tempted Christ with this question, " Master, what shall I do to inherit eternal life? " Christ asks him what was required of him " in the law? " He makes answer, " Thou shalt love the Lord thy God with all thy heart, and with all thy soul, and with all thy strength, and with all thy mind, and thy neighbour as thyself"; and Christ replies, " Thou hast answered right: this do, and thou shalt live"; as much as to say, " Do this, then thou hast fulfilled the whole law."

So in Matthew xxii., vv. 36–38, that commandment, " Thou shalt love the Lord thy God with all thy heart, and with all thy soul, and with all thy mind", is given by Christ himself as the sum of the first table of the law, in answer to the question of the lawyer, who asked Him, " Which is the great commandment in the law?"   And in the next verse, loving our neighbours as ourselves is mentioned as the sum of the second table, as it is also in Romans xiii. 9, where most of the precepts of the second table are rehearsed over in particular: " For this, Thou shalt not commit adultery, Thou shalt not kill, Thou shalt not steal, Thou shalt not bear false witness, Thou shalt not covet; and if there be any other commandment, it is briefly comprehended in this saying, namely, Thou shalt love thy neighbour as thyself."

The Apostle James seems to teach the same thing.   James ii. 8— " If ye fulfil the royal law according to the scripture, Thou shalt love thy neighbour as thyself, ye do well."

Thus frequent, express, and particular is the Scripture in teaching us that all duty is comprehended in love.   The Scripture teaches us, in like manner, of nothing else.   This is quite another thing than if religion in general had only sometimes gone under the name of the love of God, as it sometimes goes by the name of the fearing of God, and sometimes the knowledge of God, and sometimes feeling of God.

This argument does fully and irrefragably prove that all grace, and every Christian disposition and habit of mind and heart, especially as to that which is primarily holy and Divine in it, does summarily consist in Divine love, and may be resolved into it: however, with respect to its kinds and manner of exercise and its appendages, it may be diversified. For certainly there is no duty of heart, or due disposition of mind, but what is included in the " Law and the Prophets", and is required by some precept of that law and rule which He has given mankind to walk by.   But yet the Scripture affords us other evidences of the truth of this.

(2.) *The apostle speaks of Divine love as that which is the essence of all Christianity in the XIIIth chapter of* [*the*] *1st* [*Epistle to the*] *Corinthians.*   There the apostle evidently means a comparison

42

between the gifts of the Spirit and the grace of the Spirit. In the foregoing chapter the apostle had been speaking of the gifts of the Spirit throughout, such as the gift of wisdom, the gift of knowledge, the gift of faith, the gift of healing or working miracles, prophecy, discerning spirits, speaking with tongues, etc.; and in the last verse in the chapter he exhorts the Corinthians to " covet earnestly the best gifts"; but adds, " and yet shew I unto you a more excellent way", and so proceeds to discourse of the saving grace of the Spirit under the name of ἀγάπη, love, and to compare this saving grace in the heart with those gifts. Now, 'tis manifest that the comparison is between the gifts of the Spirit that were common to both saints and sinners, and that saving grace that distinguishes true saints; and, therefore, charity or love is here understood by divines as intending the same thing as sincere grace of heart.

By love or charity here there is no reason to understand the apostle [as speaking] only of love to men, but that principle of Divine love that is in the heart of the saints in the full extent, which primarily has God for its object. For there is no reason to think that the apostle doesn't mean the same thing by charity here as he does in the VIIIth chapter of the same epistle, where he is comparing the same two things together, knowledge and charity, as he does here. But there he explains himself to mean by charity the love of God: [verses 1-3]—" Now as touching things offered unto idols, we know that we all have knowledge. Knowledge puffeth up, but charity edifieth. And if any man think that he knoweth anything, he knoweth nothing yet as he ought to know. But if any man love God, the same is known of him," etc.[1]

'Tis manifest that love or charity is here (chap. xiii.) spoken of as the very essence of all Christianity, and is the very thing wherein a gracious sincerity consists. For the apostle speaks of it as the most excellent, the most necessary, and essential thing of all, without which all that makes the greatest, and fairest, and most glittering show in religion is nothing—without which, " if we speak

[1] This paragraph is an after-insertion, according to Grosart.—H.

with the tongues of men and angels, we are become as sounding brass and tinkling cymbals "—and without which, though we have " the gift of prophecy, and understand all mysteries, and all knowledge, and have all faith, so that we could remove mountains, and should bestow all our goods to feed the poor, and even give our bodies to be burned, we are nothing." Therefore, how can we understand the apostle any otherwise than that this is the very thing whereof the essence of all consists; and that he means the same by charity as a gracious charity, as indeed it is generally understood. If a man does all these things here spoken, makes such glorious prophecies, has such knowledge, such faith, and speaks so excellently, and performs such excellent external acts, and does such great things in religion as giving all his goods to the poor and giving his body to be burned, what is wanting but one thing? The very quintessence of all religion, the very thing wherein lies summarily the sincerity, spirituality, and divinity of religion. And that, the apostle teaches us, is LOVE.

And further, 'tis manifestly the apostle's drift to shew how this excellent principle does radically comprehend all that is good. For he goes on to shew how all essences of good and excellent dispositions and exercises, both towards God and towards man, are virtually contained and will flow from this one principle: " Love suffereth long, and is kind, envieth not, . . . endureth all things" etc. The words of this last verse especially respects duties to God, as the former did duties to men, as I would shew more particularly afterwards.

(Here it may be noted, by the way, that by charity " believing all things, hoping all things", the apostle has undoubtedly respect to the same faith and hope that in other parts of the chapter are mentioned together and compared with charity, [as I think might be sufficiently made manifest, if it were proper here to spend time upon it.][1] And not believing and hoping, in the case of our neigbour, which the apostle has spoken of before, in the last words of verse 5th, and had plainly summed up all parts of charity towards our neighbour in the 6th verse. And then in this verse

[1] The clause within the square-brackets is deleted in the MS.

the apostle proceeds to mention other exercises or fruits of charity quite of another kind—viz., patience under suffering, faith and hope, and perseverance.)

Thus the apostle don't only represent love or charity as the most excellent thing in Christianity, and as the quintessence, life and soul of all religion, but as that which virtually comprehends all holy virtues and exercises. And because love is the quintessence and soul of all grace, wherein the divinity and holiness of all that belongs to charity does properly and essentially consist; therefore, when Christians come to be in their most perfect state, and the Divine nature in them shall be in its greatest exaltation and purity, and be free from all mixtures, stripped of these appurtenances and that clothing that it has in the present state; and [when] it shall lose many other of its denominations, especially from the peculiar manner and exercises accommodated to the imperfect circumstances of the present state, they will be what will remain. All other names will be swallowed up in the name of charity or love, as the apostle, agreeably to his chapter on this, (1 Cor. chap. xiii.), observes in verses 8-10—" Charity never faileth. . . . But when that *which is perfect is come*, then that which is in part shall be done away." And, therefore, when the apostle, in the last verse, speaks of charity as the greatest grace, we may well understand him in the same sense as when Christ speaks of the command of love God, etc., as the greatest commandment—viz., that among the graces, that is the source and sum of all graces, as that commanded is spoken of as the sum of all commands, and requiring that duty which is the ground of all other duties.

It must be because charity is the quintessence and soul of all duty and all good in the heart that the apostle says that it is " the end of the commandment", for doubtless the main end of the commandment is to promote that which is most essential in religion and constituent of holiness.

3. *Reason bears witness to the same thing.*

(1.) *Reason testifies that Divine love is so essential in religion that all religion is but hypocrisy and a " vain show " wihout it.* What is religion but the exercise and expressions of regard to the Divine

Being? But certainly if there be no love to Him, there is no sincere regard to Him; and all pretences and show of respect to Him, whether it be in word or deed, must be hypocrisy, and of no value in the eyes of Him who sees the heart. How manifest is it that without love there can be no true honour, no sincere praise! And how can obedience be hearty, if it be not a testimony of respect to God? The fear of God without love is no other than the fear of devils; and all that outward respect and obedience, all that resignation, that repentance and sorrow for sin, that form in religion, that outward devotion that is performed merely from such a fear without love, is all of it a practical lie, as in Psalm lxvi. 3—" . . . How terrible art thou in thy works! through the greatness of thy power shall thine enemies submit themselves unto thee." In the original it is " shall thine enemies lie unto thee " —i.e., shall yield a feigned or lying obedience and respect to Thee, when still they remain enemies in their hearts. There is never a devil in hell but what would perform all that many a man [has] performed in religion, that had no love to God; and a great deal more if they were in like circumstances and the like hope of gain by it, and be as much of a devil in this heart as he is now. The Devil once seemed to be religious from fear of torment: Luke viii. 28—" When he saw Jesus, he cried out, and fell down before him, and with a loud voice said, What have I to do with thee, Jesus, thou Son of God most high? I beseech thee, torment me not." Here is external worship. The Devil is religious; he prays—he prays in a humble posture; he falls down before Christ, he lies prostrate; he prays earnestly, he cries with a loud voice; he uses humble expressions—" I beseech Thee, torment me not"; he uses respectful, honourable, adoring expressions—" Jesus, Thou Son of God most high." Nothing was wanting but LOVE.

And with respect to duties towards men, no good offices would be accepted by men one from another, if they saw the heart, and knew they did not proceed from any respect in the heart. If a child carry it very respectfully to his father, either from a strong fear, or from hope of having the larger inheritance when his father is dead, or from the like consideration, and not at all from any respect to his father in his heart; if the child's heart were open to the view of his father, and he plainly knew that there was no real regard to him. Would the child's outward honour and obedience be acceptable to the parent? So if a wife should carry it very well to her husband, and not at all from any love to him, but from other considerations plainly seen, and certainly known by the husband, Would he at all delight in her outward respect any more than if a wooden image were contrived to make respectful motions in his presence?

If duties towards men are [to be] accepted of God as a part of religion and the service of the Divine Being, they must be performed not only with a hearty love to men, but that love must flow from regard to Him.

(2.) Reason shews *that all good dispositions and duties are wholly comprehended in, and will flow from, Divine love.* Love to God and men implies all proper respect or regard to God and men; and all proper acts and expressions of regard to both will flow from it, and therefore all duty to both. To regard God and men in our heart as we ought, and to have that nature of heart towards them that we ought, is the same thing. And, therefore, a proper regard or love comprehends all virtue of heart; and he that shews all proper regard to God and men in his practice, performs all that in practice towards them which is his duty. The apostle says, Romans. xiii. 10—"Love works no ill to his neighbour." 'Tis evident by his reasoning in that place, that he means more than is expressed—that love works no ill but all good, all our duty to our neighbour: which reason plainly shews. And as the apostle teaches that love to our neighbour works no ill but all good towards our neighbour; so, by a parity of reason, love to God works no ill, but all our duty towards God.

A Christian love to God, and Christian love to men, are not properly two distinct principles in the heart. These varieties are radically the same; the same principle flowing forth towards different objects, according to the order of their existence. God is the first cause of all things, and the fountain and source of all good; and men are derived from Him, having something of His image, and are the objects of His mercy. So the first and supreme object of Divine love is God; and men are loved either as the children of God or His creatures, and those that are in His image, and the objects of His mercy, or in some respects related to God, or partakers of His loveliness, or at least capable of happiness.

That love to God, and a Christian love to men, are thus but one in their root and foundation-principle in the heart, is confirmed by several passages in the First Epistle of John: chap. iii. verses 16, 17—" Hereby perceive we the love of God, because he laid down his life for us: and we ought to lay down our lives for the brethren. But whoso hath this world's goods, . . . how dwelleth the love of God in him?" Chap. iv. 20, 21—" If a man say, I love God, and hateth his brother, he is a liar: for he that loveth not his brother whom he hath seen, how can he love God whom he hath not seen? And this commandment have we from him, That he who loveth God love his brother also." Chap. v. 1, 2—" Whosoever believeth that Jesus is the Christ is born of God: and every one that loveth Him that begat, loveth him also that is begotten of him. By this we know that we love the children of God, when we love God, and keep his commandments."

Therefore to explain the nature of Divine love, what is principally requisite is to explain the nature of love to God. For this may especially be called Divine love; and herein all Christian love or charity does radically consist, for this is the fountain of all.

As to a definition of Divine love, things of this nature are not properly capable of a definition. They are better felt than defined. Love is a term as clear in its signification, and that does as naturally suggest to the mind the thing signified by it, as any other term or terms that we can find out or substitute in its room. But yet there may be a great deal of benefit in descriptions that may be given of this heavenly principle though they all are imperfect. They may serve to limit the signification of the term and distinguish this principle from other things, and to exclude counterfeits, and also more clearly to explain some things that do appertain to its nature.

Divine love, as it has God for its object, may be thus described.

'Tis the soul's relish of the supreme excellency of the Divine nature, inclining the heart to God as the chief good.

The first thing in Divine love, and that from which everything that appertains to it arises, is a relish of the excellency of the Divine nature; which the soul of man by nature has nothing of.

The first effect that is produced in the soul, whereby it is carried above what it has or can have by nature, is to cause it to relish or taste the sweetness of the Divine relation. That is the first and most fundamental thing in Divine love, and that from which everything else that belongs to Divine love naturally and necessarily proceeds. When once the soul is brought to relish the excellency of the Divine nature, then it will naturally, and of course, incline to God every way. It will incline to be with Him and to enjoy Him. It will have benevolence to God. It will be glad that He is happy. It will incline that He should be glorified, and that His will should be done in all things. So that the first effect of the power of God in the heart in REGENERATION, is to give the heart a Divine taste or sense; to cause it to have a relish of the loveliness and sweetness of the supreme excellency of the Divine nature; and indeed this is all the immediate effect of the Divine power that there is, this is all the Spirit of God needs to do, in order to a production of all good effects in the soul. If God, by an immediate act of His, gives the soul a relish of the excellency of His own nature, other things will follow of themselves without any further act of the Divine power than only what is necessary to uphold the nature of the faculties of the soul. He that is once brought to see, or rather to taste, the superlative loveliness of the Divine Being, will need no more to make him long after the enjoyment of God, to make him rejoice in the happiness of God, and to desire that this supremely excellent Being may be pleased and glorified. (Love is commonly distinguished into a love of complacence and love of benevolence. Of these two a love of complacence is first, and is the foundation of the other,—*i.e.*, if by a love of complacence be meant a relishing a sweetness in the qualifications of the beloved, and a being pleased and delighted in his excellency. This, in the order of nature, is before benevolence, because it is the foundation and reason of it. A person must first relish that wherein the amiableness of nature consists, before he can wish well to him on the account of that loveliness, or as being worthy to receive good. Indeed, sometimes love of complacence is explained something differently, even for that joy that the soul has in the presence and possession of the beloved, which is different from the soul's relish of the beauty of the beloved, and is a fruit of it, as benevolence is. The soul may relish the sweetness and the beauty of a beloved object, whether that object be present or absent, whether in possession or not in possession; and this relish is the foundation of love of benevolence, or desire of the good of the beloved. And it is the foundation of love of affection to the beloved object when absent; and it is the foundation of one's rejoicing in the object when present; and so it is the foundation of everything else that belongs to Divine love.) And if this be true, then the main ground of true love to God is the excellency of His own nature, and not any benefit we have received, or hope to receive, by His goodness to us. Not but that there is such a thing as a gracious gratitude to God for mercies bestowed upon us; and the acts and fruits of His goodness to us may [be], and very often are, occasions and incitements of the exercise of true love to God, as I must shew more particularly hereafter. But love or affection to God, that has no other good than only some benefit received or hoped for from God, is not true love. [If it be] without any sense of a delight in the absolute excellency of the Divine nature, [it] has nothing Divine in it. Such gratitude towards God requires no more to be in the soul than that human nature that all men are born with, or at least that human nature well cultivated and improved, or indeed not further vitiated and depraved than it naturally is. It is possible that natural men, without the addition of any further principle than they have by nature, may be affected with gratitude by some remarkable kindness of God to them, as that they should be so affected with some great act of kindness of a neighbour. A principle of self-love is all that is necessary to both. But Divine love is a principle distinct from self-love, and from all that arises from it. Indeed, after a man is come to relish the sweetness of the supreme good there is in the nature of God, self-love may have a hand in an appetite after the enjoyment of that good. For self-love will necessarily make a man desire to enjoy that which is sweet to him. But God's perfections must first savour appetite and [be] sweet to men, or they must first have a taste to relish sweetness in the perfection of God, before self-love can have any influence upon them to cause an appetite after the enjoyment of that sweetness. And therefore that divine taste or relish of the soul, wherein Divine love doth most fundamentally consist, is prior to all influence that self-love can have to incline us to God; and so must be a principle quite distinct from it, and independent of it.

III

SHEWING HOW A PRINCIPLE OF GRACE IS FROM THE SPIRIT OF GOD

I. *That this holy and Divine principle, which we have shewn does radically and summarily consist in Divine love, comes into existence in the soul by the power of God in the influences of the Holy Spirit, the third Person in the blessed Trinity, is abundantly manifest from the Scriptures.*

Regeneration is by the Spirit: John iii. 5, 6—"Verily, verily, I say unto thee, Except a man be born of water, and of the Spirit, he cannot enter into the kingdom of God. That which is born of the flesh is flesh; and that which is born of the Spirit is spirit." And verse 8—" The wind bloweth where it listeth, and thou hearest the sound thereof, but canst not tell whence it cometh, and whither it goeth: so is every one that is born of the Spirit."

The renewing of the soul is by the Holy Ghost: Titus iii. 5—" Not by works of righteousness which we have done, but according to his mercy he saved us, by the washing of regeneration, and renewing of the Holy Ghost." A new heart is given by God's putting His Spirit within us: Ezekiel xxxvi. 26, 27—" A new heart also will I give you, and a new spirit will I put within you; and I will take away the stony heart out of your flesh, and I will give

you an heart of flesh. And I will put my Spirit within you, and
cause you to walk in my statutes, and ye shall keep my judgments
and do them." Quickening of the dead soul is by the Spirit:
John vi. 63—" It is the Spirit that quickeneth." Sanctification is
by the Spirit of God: 2 Thess. ii. 13—" God hath from the beginning chosen you to salvation through sanctification of the Spirit
and belief of the truth." Romans xv. 16—" That the offering up
of the Gentiles might be acceptable, being sanctified by the Holy
Ghost." 1 Cor. vi. 11—" Such were some of you: but ye are
washed, but ye are sanctified, but ye are justified in the name of the
Lord Jesus, and by the Spirit of our God." 1 Peter i. 2—" Elect
according to the foreknowledge of God the Father, through
sanctification of the Spirit, unto obedience and sprinkling of the
blood of Jesus Christ." All grace in the heart is the fruit of the
Spirit: Gal. v. 22, 23—" But the fruit of the Spirit is love, joy,
peace, long-suffering, gentleness, goodness, faith, meekness, temperance." Eph. v. 9—" The fruit of the Spirit is in all goodness
and righteousness and truth." Hence the Spirit of God is called
the Spirit of grace, (Heb. x. 29).

   This doctrine of a gracious nature being by the immediate influence of the Spirit of God, is not only taught in the Scriptures, but
is irrefragable to reason. Indeed there seems to be a strong disposition in men to disbelieve and oppose the doctrine of true
disposition, to disbelieve and oppose the doctrine of immediate
influence of the Spirit of God in the hearts of men, or to diminish
and make it as small and remote a matter as possible, and put it as
far out of sight as may be. Whereas it seems to me, true virtue
and holiness would naturally excite a prejudice (if I may say) in
favour of such a doctrine; and that the soul, when in the most
excellent frame, and the most lively exercise of virtue,—love to
God and delight in Him,—would naturally and unavoidably think
of God as kindly communicating Himself to him, and holding
communion with him, as though he did as it were see God smiling
on him, giving to him and conversing with him; and that if he did
not so think of God, but, on the contrary, should conceive that
there was no immediate communication between God and him,

it would tend greatly to quell his holy motions of soul, and be an exceeding damage to his pleasure.

No good reason can be given why men should have such an inward disposition to deny any immediate communication between God and the creature, or to make as little of it as possible. 'Tis a strange disposition that men have to thrust God out of the world, or to put Him as far out of sight as they can, and to have in no respect immediately and sensibly to do with Him. Therefore so many schemes have been drawn to exclude, or extenuate, or remove at a great distance, any influence of the Divine Being in the hearts of men, such as the scheme of the Pelagians, the Socinians, etc. And therefore these doctrines are so much ridiculed that ascribe much to the immediate influence of the Spirit, and called enthusiasm, fanaticism, whimsy, and distraction; but no mortal can tell for what.

If we make no difficulty of allowing that God did immediately make the whole universe at first, and caused it to exist out of nothing, and that every individual thing owes its being to an immediate, voluntary, arbitrary act of almighty power, why should we make a difficulty of supposing that He has still something immediately to do with the things that He has made, and that there is an arbitrary influence still that God has in the creation that He has made?

And if it be reasonable to suppose it with respect to any part of the creation, it is especially so with respect to reasonable creatures, who are the highest part of the creation, next to God, and who are most immediately made for God, and have Him for their next head, and are created for the business wherein they are mostly concerned. And above all, in that wherein the highest excellency of this highest rank of beings consist, and that wherein he is most conformed to God, is nearest to Him, and has God for his most immediate object.

It seems to me most rational to suppose that as we ascend in the order of being we shall at last come immediately to God, the first cause. In whatever respect we ascend, we ascend in the order of time and succession.

II. *The Scripture speaks of this holy and Divine principle in the heart as not only from the Spirit, but as being spiritual.* Thus saving knowledge is called spiritual understanding: Col. i. 9—" We desire that ye might be filled with the knowledge of his will in all wisdom and spiritual understanding." So the influences, graces, and comforts of God's Spirit are called spiritual blessings: Eph. i. 3— "Blessed be the God and Father of our Lord Jesus Christ, who hath blessed us with all spiritual blessings in heavenly places in Christ." So the imparting of any gracious benefit is called the imparting of a spiritual gift: Rom. i. 11—" For I long to see you, that I may impart unto you some spiritual gift." And the fruits of the Spirit which are offered to God are called spiritual sacrifices: 1 Peter ii. 5—" An holy priesthood to offer up spiritual sacrifices, acceptable to God by Jesus Christ." And a spiritual person signifies the same in Scripture as a gracious person, and sometimes one that is much under the influence of grace: 1 Cor. ii. 15—" He that is spiritual judgeth all things, yet he himself is judged of no man "; and iii. 1—" And I, brethren, could not speak unto you as unto spiritual but as unto carnal." Gal. vi. 1— " If a man be overtaken in a fault, ye which are spiritual restore such an one in the spirit of meekness." And to be graciously minded is called in Scripture a being spiritually minded: Rom. viii. 6—" To be spiritually minded is life and peace."

Concerning this, two things are to be noted.

1. *That this Divine principle in the heart is not called spiritual, because it has its seat in the soul or spiritual part of man, and not in his body.* It is called spiritual, not because of its relation to the spirit of man, in which it is, but because of its relation to the Spirit of God, from which it is. That things are not called spiritual because they appertain not to the body but the spirit of man is evident, because gracious or holy understanding is called spiritual understanding in the forementioned passage, (Col. i. 9). Now, by spiritual understanding cannot be meant that understanding which has its seat in the soul, to distinguish it from other understanding that has its seat in the body, for all understanding has its seat in the soul; and that things are called spiritual because of

their relation to the Spirit of God is most plain, by the latter part of the 2d chapter of 1st Corinthians. There we have both those expressions, one immediately after another, evidently meaning the same thing: verses 13, 14—" Which things also we speak, not in the words which man's wisdom teacheth, but which the Holy Ghost teacheth; comparing spiritual things with spiritual. But the natural man receiveth not the things of the Spirit of God." And that by the spiritual man is meant one that has the Spirit is also as plainly evident by the context: verses 10-12—" God hath revealed *them* unto us by his Spirit: for the Spirit searcheth all things, yea, the deep things of God. For what man knoweth the things of a man," etc. Also ver. 15—"He that is spiritual judgeth all things", by which is evidently meant the same as he that hath the Spirit that " searcheth all things", as we find in the forgoing verses. So persons are said to be spiritually minded, not because they mind things that relate to the soul or spirit of man, but because they mind things that relate to the Spirit of God: Romans viii. 5, 6—" For they that are after the flesh do mind the things of the flesh; but they that are after the Spirit the things of the Spirit. For to be carnally minded is death; but to be spiritually minded is life and peace."

2. *It must be observed that where this holy Divine principle of saving grace wrought in the mind is in Scripture called spiritual, what is intended by the expression is not merely nor chiefly that it is from the Spirit of God, but that it is of the nature of the Spirit of God.* There are many things in the minds of some natural men that are from the influence of the Spirit, but yet are by no means spiritual things in the scriptural sense of the word. The Spirit of God convinces natural men of sin, (John xvi. 8). Natural men may have common grace, common illuminations, and common affections that are from the Spirit of God, as appears by Hebrews vi. 4. Natural men have sometimes the influences of the Spirit of God in His common operations and gifts, and therefore God's Spirit is said to be striving with them, and they are said to resist the Spirit, (Acts vii. 51); to grieve and vex God's Holy Spirit, (Eph. iv. 30; Isaiah lxiii. 10); and God is

said to depart from them even as the Spirit of the Lord departed from Saul: 1 Sam. xvi. 14—" But the Spirit of the Lord departed from Saul, and an evil spirit from the Lord troubled him."

But yet natural men are not in any degree spiritual. The great difference between natural men and godly men seems to be set forth by this, that the one is natural and carnal, and the other spiritual; and natural men are so totally destitute of that which is Spirit, that they know nothing about it, and the reason given for it is because they are not spiritual, (1 Cor. ii. 13-15.) Indeed sometimes those miraculous gifts of the Spirit that were common are called spiritual because they are from the Spirit of God; but for the most part the term seems to be appropriate to its gracious influences and fruits on the soul, which are no otherwise spiritual than the common influences of the Spirit that natural men have, in any other respect than this, that this saving grace in the soul, is not only from the Spirit, but it also partakes of the nature of that Spirit that it is from, which the common grace of the Spirit does not. Thus things in Scripture language are said to be earthly, as they partake of an earthly nature, partake of the nature of the earth; so things are said to be heavenly, as they in their nature agree with those things that are in heaven; and so saving grace in the heart is said to be spiritual, and therein distinguished from all other influences of the Spirit, that it is of the nature of the Spirit of God. It partakes of the nature of that Spirit, while no common gift of the Spirit doth so.

But here an enquiry may be raised, viz. :—

Enq. *How does saving grace partake of the nature of that Spirit that it is from, so as to be called on that account spiritual, thus essentially distinguishing it from all other effects of the Spirit ?* for every effect has in some respect or another the nature of its cause, and the common convictions and illuminations that natural men have are in some respects [of] the nature of the Spirit of God; for there is light and understanding and conviction of truth in these common illuminations, and so they are of the nature of the Spirit of God—that is, a discerning spirit and a spirit of truth. But yet saving grace, by its being called spiritual, as though it were thereby distinguished from all other gifts of the Spirit, seems to partake of the nature of the Spirit of God in some very peculiar manner.

Clearly to satisfy this enquiry, we must do these two things:— 1. We must bear in mind what has already been said of the nature of saving grace, and what I have already shewn to be that wherein its nature and essence lies, and wherein all saving grace is radically and summarily comprised—viz., a principle of Divine love. 2. We must consider what the Scripture reveals to be in a peculiar manner the nature of the Holy Spirit of God, and in an enquiry of this nature I would go no further than I think the Scripture plainly goes before me. The Word of God certainly should be our rule in matters so much above reason and our own notions.

And here I would say—

(1.) That I think *the Scripture does sufficiently reveal the Holy Spirit as a proper Divine person;* and thus we ought to look upon Him as a distinct personal agent. He is often spoken of as a person, revealed under personal characters and in personal acts, and it speaks of His being acted on as a person, and the Scripture plainly ascribes every thing to Him that properly denotes a distinct person; and though the word person be rarely used in the Scriptures, yet I believe that we have no word in the English language that does so naturally represent what the Scripture reveals of the distinction of the Eternal Three,—Father, Son, and Holy Ghost,—as to say they are one God but three persons.

(2.) *Though all the Divine perfections are to be attributed to each person of the Trinity, yet the Holy Ghost is in a peculiar manner called by the name of Love*—'Αγάπη, the same word is that translated charity in the XIIIth chapter of 1st Corinthians. The Godhead or the Divine essence is once and again said to be love: 1 John iv. 8—" He that loveth not knoweth not God; for God is love." So again, ver. 16—" God is love; and he that dwelleth in love, dwelleth in God, and God in him." But the Divine essence is thus called in a peculiar manner as breathed forth and subsisting in the Holy Spirit; as may be seen in the context of these texts, as in the 12th and 13th verses of the same chapter—" No man hath seen God at any time. If we love one another, God dwelleth in us, and his love is perfected in us. Hereby know we that we dwell in him, and he in us, because he hath given us of his Spirit." It is the same argument in both these verses: in the 12th verse the apostle argues that if we have love dwelling in us, we have God dwelling in us; and in the 13th verse he clears the face of the argument by this, that his love which is dwelling in us is God's Spirit. And this shews that the foregoing argument is good, and that if love dwells in us, we know God dwells in us indeed, for the apostle supposed it as a thing granted and allowed that God's Spirit is God. The Scripture elsewhere does abundantly teach us that the way in which God dwells in the saints is by His Spirit, by their being the temples of the Holy Ghost. Here this apostle teaches us the same thing. He says, " We know that he dwelleth in us, that he hath given us his Spirit"; and this is manifestly to explain what is said in the foregoing verse—viz., that God dwells in us, inasmuch as His love dwells in us; which love he had told us before—ver. 8—is God himself. And afterwards, in the 16th verse, he expresses it more fully, that this is the way that God dwells in the saint—viz., because this love dwells in them, which is God.

Again the same is signified in the same manner in the last verses of the foregoing chapter. In the foregoing verses, speaking of love as a true sign of sincerity and our acceptance with God, beginning with the 18th verse, he sums up the argument thus in the last verse: " And hereby we know that he abideth in us, by the Spirit which he hath given us."

We have also something very much like this in the apostle Paul's writings.

Gal. v. 13-16—" Use not liberty for an occasion to the flesh, but by love serve one another. For all the law is fulfilled in one word, even in this, Thou shalt love thy neighbour as thyself. But if ye bite and devour one another, take heed that ye be not consumed one of another. This I say then, Walk in the Spirit, and ye shall not fulfil the lust of the flesh." Here it seems most evident that what the apostle exhorts and urges in the 13th, 14th, and 15th verses,—viz., that they should walk in love, that they might not give occasion to the gratifying of the flesh,—he does expressly explain in the 16th verse by this, that they should walk in the Spirit, that they might not fulfil the lust of the flesh; which the great Mr Howe[1] takes notice of in his " Sermons on the Prosperous State of the Christian Interest before the End of Time", p. 185, published by Mr Evans. His words are, " Walking in the Spirit is directed with a special eye and reference unto the exercise of this love; as you may see in Galatians v., the 14th, 15th, and 16th verses compared together. All the law is fulfilled in one word, (he means the whole law of the second table), even in this, Thou shalt love thy neighbour as thyself. But if ye bite and devour one another, (the opposite to this love, or that which follows on the want of it, or from the opposite principle), take heed that ye be not consumed one of another. This I say then, (observe the inference), Walk in the Spirit, and ye shall not fulfil the lust of the flesh. To walk in the Spirit is to walk in the exercise of this love."

So that as the Son of God is spoken of as the wisdom, understanding, and Λογος of God, (Proverbs viii. ; Luke xi. 49 ; John i., at the beginning), and is, as divines express things, the personal wisdom of God; so the Spirit of God is spoken of as the love of God, and may with equal foundation and propriety be called the personal love of God. We read in the beloved disciple's writings of these two—Λογος and 'Αγάπη, both of which are said to be God, (John i. 1 ; 1 John iv. 8-16). One is the Son of God, and the other the Holy Spirit. There are two things that God is said to be in this First Epistle of John—light and love: chap. i. 5—" God is light." This is the Son of God, who is said to be the wisdom and reason of God, and the brightness of His glory; and in the 4th chapter of the same epistle he says, " God is love", and this he applies to the Holy Spirit.

---

[1] This is John Howe (1630-1705), a life-long friend of Henry More and Ralph Cudworth, and chaplain to Oliver Cromwell. He was one of the front rank of Puritan theologians and preachers. The sermons referred to by Edwards form part of his 'posthumous works', sermon notes taken by his hearers and published after his death. Howe may be one source of Edwards platonism.—H.

Hence the Scripture symbol of the Holy Ghost is a dove, which is the emblem of love, and so was continually accounted (as is well known) in the heathen world, and is so made use of by their poets and mythologists, which probably arose partly from the nature and manner of the bird, and probably in part from the tradition of the story of Noah's dove, that came with a message of peace and love after such terrible manifestations of God's wrath in the time of the deluge. This bird is also made use of as an emblem of love in the Holy Scriptures; as it was on that message of peace and love that God sent it to Noah, when it came with an olive-leaf in its mouth, and often in Solomon's Song: Cant. i. 15—" Thou hast doves' eyes ": Cant. v. 12— " His eyes are as the eyes of doves ": Cant. v. 2—" Open to me, my love, my dove ", and in other places in that song.

This bird, God is pleased to choose as the special symbol of His Holy Spirit in the greatest office or work of the Spirit that ever it has or will exert—viz., in anointing Christ, the great Head of the whole Church of saints, from which Head this holy oil descends to all the members, and the skirts of His garments, as the sweet and precious ointment that was poured on Aaron's head, that great type of Christ. As God the Father then poured forth His Holy Spirit of love upon the Son without measure, so that which was then seen with the eye—viz., a dove descending and lighting upon Christ—signified the same thing as what was at the same time proclaimed to the Son—viz., This is my beloved Son, in whom I am well pleased. This is the Son on whom I pour forth all my love, towards whom my essence entirely flows out in love. See Matt. iii. 16, 17; Mark i. 10, 11; Luke iii. 22; John i. 32, 33.

This was the anointing of the Head of the Church and our great High Priest, and therefore the holy anointing oil of old with which Aaron and other typical high priests were anointed was the most eminent type of the Holy Spirit of any in the Old Testament. This holy oil, by reason of its soft-flowing and diffusive nature, and its unparalleled sweetness and fragrancy, did most fitly represent Divine love, or that Spirit that is the

deity, breathed forth or flowing out and softly falling in infinite
love and delight. It is mentioned as a fit representation of holy
love, which is said to be like the precious ointment on the head,'
that ran down upon the beard, even Aaron's beard, that went
down to the skirts of his garments. It was from the fruit of the
olive-tree, which it is known has been made use of as a symbol
of love or peace, which was probably taken from the olive-branch
brought by the dove to Noah in token of the Divine favour; so
that the olive-branch and the dove that brought it, both signified
the same thing—viz., love, which is specially typified by the
precious oil from the olive-tree.

God's love is primarily to Himself, and His infinite delight is in
Himself, in the Father and the Son loving and delighting in each
other. We often read of the Father loving the Son, and being
well pleased in the Son, and of the Son loving the Father. In the
infinite love and delight that is between these two persons consists the infinite happiness of God: Prov. viii. 30.—" Then I was
by him, as one brought up with him: and I was daily his delight,
rejoicing always before him "; and therefore seeing the Scripture
signifies that the Spirit of God is the love of God, therefore it
follows that Holy Spirit proceeds from or is breathed forth from,
the Father and the Son in some way or other infinitely above all
our conceptions, as the Divine essence entirely flows out and is
breathed forth in infinitely pure love and sweet delight from the
Father and the Son; and this is that pure river of water of life
that proceeds out of the throne of the Father and the Son, as we
read at the beginning of the XXII^d chapter of the Revelation;
for Christ himself tells us that by the water of life, or living
water, is meant the Holy Ghost, (John vii. 38, 39). This river of
water of life in the Revelation is evidently the same with the
living waters of the sanctuary in Ezekiel, (Ezek. xlvii. 1, etc.); and
this river is doubtless the river of God's pleasure, or of God's own
infinite delight spoken of in Ps. xxxvi. 7–9—" How excellent is
thy loving-kindness, O God! therefore the children of men put
their trust under the shadow of thy wings. They shall be abundantly satisfied with the fatness of thy house; and thou shalt make

them drink of the river of thy pleasures. For with thee is the fountain of life." The river of God's pleasures here spoken of is the same with the fountain of life spoken of in the next words. Here, as was observed before, the water of life by Christ's own interpretation is the Holy Spirit. This river of God's pleasures is also the same with the fatness of God's house, the holy oil of the sanctuary spoken of in the next preceding words, and is the same with God's love, or God's excellent loving-kindness, spoken of in the next preceding verse.

I have before observed that the Scripture abundantly reveals that the way in which Christ dwells in the saint is by His Spirit's dwelling in them, and here I would observe that Christ in His prayer, in the XVIIth chapter of John, seems to speak of the way in which He dwells in them as by the indwelling of the love wherewith the Father has loved Him: John xvii. 26—" And I have declared unto them thy name, and will declare it; that the love wherewith thou hast loved me may be in them, and I in them." The beloved disciple that wrote this Gospel having taken [such] particular notice of this, that he afterwards in his first epistle once and again speaks of love's dwelling in the saints, and the Spirit's dwelling in them being the same thing.

Again, the Scripture seems in many places to speak of love in Christians as if it were the same with the Spirit of God in them, or at least as the prime and most natural breathing and acting of the Spirit in the soul. So Rom. v. 5—" Because the love of God is shed abroad in our hearts by the Holy Ghost, which is given unto us": Col. i. 8—" Who also declared unto us your love in the Spirit": 2 Cor. vi. 6—" By kindness, by the Holy Ghost, by love unfeigned ": Phil. ii. 1—" If there be therefore any consolation in Christ, if any comfort of love, if any fellowship of the Spirit, if any bowels and mercies, fulfil ye my joy, that ye be like-minded, having the same love, being of one accord, of one mind."

The Scripture therefore leads us to this conclusion, though it be infinitely above us to conceive how it should be, that yet as the Son of God is the personal word, idea, or wisdom of God, begotten by God, being an infinitely perfect, substantial image or idea of Himself, (as might be very plainly proved from the Holy Scripture, if here were proper occasion for it); so the Holy Spirit does in some ineffable and inconceivable manner proceed, and is breathed forth both from the Father and the Son, by the Divine essence being wholly poured and flowing out in that infinitely intense, holy, and pure love and delight that continually and unchangeably breathes forth from the Father and the Son, primarily towards each other, and secondarily towards the creature, and so flowing forth in a different subsistence or person in a manner to us utterly inexplicable and inconceivable, and that this is that person that is poured forth into the hearts of angels and saints.

Hence 'tis to be accounted for, that though we often read in Scripture of the Father loving the Son, and the Son loving the Father, yet we never once read either of the Father or the Son loving the Holy Spirit, and the Spirit loving either of them. It is because the Holy Spirit is the Divine love itself, the love of the Father and the Son. Hence also it is to be accounted for, that we very often read of the love both of the Father and the Son to men, and particularly their love to the saints; but we never read of the Holy Ghost loving them, for the Holy Ghost is that love of God and Christ that is breathed forth primarily towards each other, and flows out secondarily towards the creature. This also will well account for it, that the apostle Paul so often wishes grace, mercy, and peace from God the Father, and from the Lord Jesus Christ, in the beginning of his epistles, without even mentioning the Holy Ghost, because the Holy Ghost is Himself the love and grace of God the Father and the Lord Jesus Christ. He is the deity wholly breathed forth in infinite, substantial, intelligent love: from the Father and Son first towards each other, and secondarily freely flowing out to the creature, and so standing forth a distinct personal subsistence.

Both the holiness and happiness of the Godhead consists in this love. As we have already proved, all creature holiness consists essentially and summarily in love to God and love to other creatures; so does the holiness of God consist in His love, especially in the perfect and intimate union and love there is between the Father and the Son. But the Spirit that proceeds from the Father and the Son is the bond of this union, as it is of all holy union between the Father and the Son, and between God and the creature, and between the creatures among themselves. All seems to be signified in Christ's prayer in the XVIIth chapter of John, from the 21st verse. Therefore this Spirit of love is the " bond of perfectness " (Col. iii. 14) throughout the whole blessed society or family in heaven and earth, consisting of the Father, the head of the family, and the Son, and all His saints that are the disciples, seed, and spouse of the Son. The happiness of God doth also consist in this love; for doubtless the happiness of God consists in the infinite love He has to, and delight He has in Himself; or in other words, in the infinite delight there is between the Father and the Son, spoken of in Prov. viii. 30. This delight that the Father and the Son have in each other is not to be distinguished from their love of complacence one in another, wherein love does most essentially consist, as was observed before. The happiness of the deity, as all other true happiness, consists in love and society.

Hence it is the Spirit of God, the third Person in the Trinity, is so often called the Holy Spirit, as though " holy " were an epithet some way or other peculiarly belonging to Him, which can be no other way than that the holiness of God does consist in Him. He is not only infinitely holy as the Father and the Son are, but He is the holiness of God itself in the abstract. The holiness of the Father and the Son does consist in breathing forth this Spirit. Therefore He is not only called the Holy Spirit, but the Spirit of holiness: Rom. i. 4—" According to the Spirit of holiness."

Hence also the river of " living waters", or waters of life, which Christ explains in the VIIth [chapter] of John, of the Holy Spirit, is in the forementioned Psalm [xxxvi. 8] called the " river of God's pleasures "; and hence also that holy oil with which Christ was anointed, which I have shewn was the Holy Ghost, is called the

" oil of gladness ": Heb. i. 9—" Therefore God, even thy God, hath anointed thee with the oil of gladness above thy fellows." Hence we learn that God's fulness does consist in the Holy Spirit. By fulness, as the term is used in Scripture, as may easily be seen by looking over the texts that mention it, is intended the good that any one possesses. Now the good that God possesses does most immediately consist in His joy and complacence that He has in Himself. It does objectively, indeed, consist in the Father and the Son; but it doth most immediatly consist in the complacence in these elements. Nevertheless the fulness of God consists in the holiness and happiness of the deity. Hence persons, by being made partakers of the Holy Spirit, or having it dwelling in them, are said to be " partakers of the fulness of God " or Christ. Christ's fulness, as mediator, consists in His having the Spirit given Him " not by measure", (John iii. 34.) And so it is that He is said to have " the fulness of the Godhead", [which] is said " to dwell in him bodily", (Col. ii. 9.) And as we, by receiving the Holy Spirit from Christ, and being made partakers of His Spirit, are said " to receive of his fulness, and grace for grace." And because this Spirit, which is the fulness of God, consists in the love of God and Christ; therefore we, by knowing the love of Christ, are said " to be filled with all the fulness of God", (Eph. iii. 19). For the way that we know the love of Christ, is by having that love dwelling in us, as 1 John iv. 13; because the fulness of God consists in the Holy Spirit. Hence our communion with God the Father and God the Son consists in our possessing of the Holy Ghost, which is their Spirit. For to have communion or fellowship with either, is to partake with them of their good in their fulness in union and society with them. Hence it is that we read of the saints having fellowship and communion with the Father and with the Son; but never of their having fellowship with the Holy Ghost, because the Holy Ghost is that common good or fulness which they partake of, in which their fellowship consists. We read of the communion of the Holy Ghost; but not of communion with Him, which are two very different things.

Persons are said to have communion with each other when they partake with each other in some common good; but any one is said to have communion of anything, with respect to that thing they partake of, in common with others. Hence, in the apostolical benediction, he wishes the " grace of the Lord Jesus Christ, and the love of God the Father, and the communion or partaking of the Holy Ghost." The blessing wished is but one—viz., the Holy Spirit. To partake of the Holy Ghost is to have that love of the Father and the grace of the Son.

From what has been said, it follows that the Holy Spirit is the *summum* of all good. 'Tis the fulness of God. The holiness and happiness of the Godhead consists in it; and in communion or partaking of it consists all the true loveliness and happiness of the creature. All the grace and comfort that persons here have, and all their holiness and happiness hereafter, consists in the love of the Spirit, spoken of Rom. xv. 30; and joy in the Holy Ghost, spoken of Rom. xiv. 17; Acts ix. 31, xiii. 52. And, therefore, that which in Matt. vii. 11—" If ye then, being evil, know how to give good gifts unto your children, how much more shall your Father which is in heaven, give good things to them that ask him! "—is in Luke xi. 13, expressed thus:—" If ye then, being evil, know how to give good gifts unto your children; how much more shall your heavenly Father give the Holy Spirit to them that ask him?" Doubtless there is an agreement in what is expressed by each evangelist: and giving the Holy Spirit to them that ask, is the same as giving good things to them that ask; for the Holy Spirit is the sum of all good.

Hence we may better understand the economy of the persons of the Trinity as it appears in the part that each one has in the affair of redemption, and shews the equality of each Person concerned in that affair, and the equality of honour and praise due to each of them. For that work, glory belongs to the Father and the Son, that they so greatly loved the world. To the Father, that He so loved the world, that He gave His only-begotten Son, who was all His delight, who is His infinite objective happiness. To the Son, that He so loved the world, that He gave Himself. But there is equal glory due to the Holy Ghost on this account, because He is the love of the Father and the Son, that flows out primarily towards God, and secondarily towards the elect that Christ came to save. So that, however wonderful the love of the Father and the Son appear to be, so much the more glory belongs to the Holy Spirit, in whom subsists that wonderful and excellent love.

It shews the infinite excellency of the Father thus:—that the Son so delighted in Him, and prized His honour and glory, that when He had a mind to save sinners, He came infinitely low, rather than men's salvation should be the injury of that honour and glory. It shewed the infinite excellency and worth of the Son, that the Father so delighted in Him, that for His sake He was ready to quit His own; yea, and receive into favour those that had deserved infinitely ill at His hands. Both shews the infinite excellency of the Holy Spirit, because He is that delight of the Father and the Son in each other, which is manifested to be so great and infinite by these things.

What has been said shews that our dependence is equally on each person in this affair. The Father approves and provides the redeemer, and Himself accepts the price of the good purchased, and bestows that good. The Son is the redeemer, and the price that is offered for the purchased good. And the Holy Ghost is the good purchased; [for] the sacred Scriptures seem to intimate that the Holy Spirit is the sum of all that Christ purchased for man, (Gal. iii. 13, 14.)

What Christ purchased for us is, that we might have communion with God in His good, which consists in partaking or having communion of the Holy Ghost, as I have shewn. All the blessedness of the redeemed consists in partaking of the fulness of Christ, their head and redeemer, which, I have observed, consists in partaking of the Spirit that is given Him not by measure. This is the vital sap which the creatures derive from the true vine. This is the holy oil poured on the head, that goes down to the members. Christ purchased for us that we should enjoy the love: but the love of God flows out in the proceeding of the Spirit;

and He purchased for them that the love and joy of God should dwell in them, which is by the indwelling of the Holy Spirit.

The sum of all spiritual good which the saints have in this world, is that spring of living water within them which we read of, (John iv. 10); and those rivers of living waters flowing from within them which we read of, (John vii. 38, 39), which we are there told is the Holy Spirit. And the sum of all happiness in the other world, is that river of living water which flows from the throne of God and the Lamb, which is the river of God's pleasures, and is the Holy Spirit, which is often compared in sacred Scripture to water, to the rain and dew, and rivers and floods of waters, (Isa. xliv. 3, xxxii. 15, xli. 17, 18, compared with John iv. 14, Isa. xxxv. 6, 7, xliii. 19, 20.)

The Holy Spirit is the purchased possession and inheritance of the saints, as appears, because that little of it which the saints have in this world is said to be the earnest of that purchased inheritance, (Eph. i. 13, 14; 2 Cor. i. 22,). 'Tis an earnest of that which we are to have a fulness of hereafter. The Holy Ghost is the great subject of all gospel promises, and therefore is called the Spirit of promise, (Eph. i. 13). He is called the promise of the Father, (Luke xxiv. 49).

The Holy Ghost being a comprehension of all good things promised in the gospel, we may easily see the force of the Apostle's inquiry: Gal. iii. 2—" This only would I learn of you Received ye the Spirit by the works of the law, or by the hearing of faith? " So that in the offer of redemption 'tis of God of whom our good is purchased, and 'tis God that purchases it, and 'tis God also that is the thing purchased. Thus all our good things are of God, and through God, and in God, as Rom. xi. 36—" For of him, and through him, and to him, and in him, [as εἰς is rendered in 1 Cor. viii. 6], are all things: to whom be glory for ever." All our good is of God the Father, and through God the Son, and all is in the Holy Ghost, as He is Himself all our good. And so God is Himself the portion and purchased inheritance of His people. Thus God is the Alpha and Omega in this affair of redemption.

If we suppose no more than used to be supposed about the Holy

Ghost, the honour of the Holy Ghost in the work of redemption is not equal in any sense to the Father and the Son's; nor is there an equal part of the glory of this work belonging to Him. Merely to apply to us, or immediately to give or hand to us blessing purchased, after it is purchased, is subordinate to the other two Persons,—is but a little thing to the purchaser of it by the paying an infinite price by Christ, by Christ's offering up Himself a sacrifice to procure it; and 'tis but a little thing to God the Father's giving His infinitely dear Son to be a sacrifice for us to procure this good. But according to what has now been supposed, there is an equality. To be the wonderful love of God, is as much as for the Father and the Son to exercise wonderful love; and to be the thing purchased, is as much as to be the price that purchases it. The price, and the thing bought with that price, answer each other in value; and to be the excellent benefit offered, is as much as to offer such an excellent benefit. For the glory that belongs to Him that bestows the gospel, arises from the excellency and value of the gift, and therefore the glory is equal to that excellency of the benefit. And so that person that is that excellent benefit, has equal glory with Him that bestows such an excellent benefit.

But now to return: from what has been now observed from the Holy Scriptures of the nature of the Holy Spirit, may be clearly understood why grace in the hearts of the saints is called spiritual, in distinction from other things that are the effects of the Spirit in the hearts of men. For by this it appears that the Divine principle in the saints is of the nature of the Spirit; for as the nature of the Spirit of God is Divine love, so Divine love is the nature and essence of that holy principle in the hearts of the saints.

The Spirit of God may operate and produce effects upon the minds of natural men that have no grace, as He does when He assists natural conscience and convictions of sin and danger. The Spirit of God may produce effects upon inanimate things, as of old He moved on the face of the waters. But He communicates holiness in His own proper nature only, in those holy effects in the hearts of the saints. And, therefore, those holy effects only are called spiritual; and the saints only are called spiritual persons in sacred Scripture.

Men's natural faculties and principles may be assisted by the operation of the Spirit of God on their minds, to enable them to exert those acts which, to a greater or lesser degree, they exert naturally. But the Spirit don't at all communicate Himself in it in His own nature, which is Divine love, any more than when He moved upon the face of the waters.

Hence also we may more easily receive and understand a doctrine that seems to be taught us in the sacred Scripture concerning grace in the heart—viz., that it is no other than the Spirit of God itself dwelling and acting in the heart of a saint,—which the consideration of these things will make manifest:—

(1.) That the sacred Scriptures don't only call grace spiritual, but " spirit."

(2.) That when the sacred Scriptures call grace spirit, the Spirit of God is intended; and that grace is called "spirit" no otherwise than as the name of the Holy Ghost, the third person in the Trinity is ascribed to it.

1. This holy principle is often called by the name of " spirit " in sacred Scripture. So in John iii. 6—" That which is born of the Spirit is spirit." Here by flesh and spirit, we have already shewn, are intended those two opposite principles in the heart, corruption and grace. So by flesh and spirit the same things are manifestly intended in Gal. v. 17—" For the flesh lusteth against the Spirit, and the Spirit against the flesh: and these are contrary the one to the other; so that ye cannot do the things that ye would." This that is here given as the reason why Christians cannot do the things that they would, is manifestly the same that is given for the same thing in the latter part of the VIIth chapter of the Romans. The reason there given why they cannot do the things that they would is, that the law of the members war with [and] against the law of the mind; and, therefore, by the law of the members and the law of the mind are meant the same as the flesh and Spirit in Galatians. Yea, they are called by the same name of the flesh and Spirit there, in that context, in the continu-

ation of the same discourse in the beginning of the next chapter:—
" Therefore there is no condemnation to them that are in Christ
Jesus, that walk not after the flesh, but after the Spirit." Here
the apostle evidently refers to the same two opposite principles
warring one against another, that he had been speaking of in the
close of the preceding chapter, which he here calls flesh and
Spirit as he does in his Epistle to the Galatians.

This is yet more abundantly clear by the next words, which
are, " For the law of the Spirit of life in Christ Jesus hath made me
free from the law of sin and death." Here these two things that
in the preceding verse are called " flesh and Spirit", are in this
verse called " the law of the Spirit of life " and " the law of sin
and death", evidently speaking still of the same law of our mind
and the law of sin spoken of in the last verse of the preceding
chapter. The Apostle goes on in the VIIIth chapter to call aversa-
tion and grace by the names of flesh and Spirit, (verses 5-9, and
again verses 12, 13). These two principles are called by the same
names in Matt. xxvi. 41—" The spirit indeed is willing, but the
flesh is weak." There can be no doubt but that the same thing is
intended here by the flesh and spirit as (compare what is said of
the flesh and spirit here and in these places) in the VIIth and VIIIth
chapters of Romans, and Gal. V. Again, these two principles
are called by the same words in Gal. vi. 8. If this be compared
with the 18th verse of the foregoing chapter, and with Romans
viii. 6 and 13, none can doubt but the same is meant in each place.

2. If the sacred Scriptures be duly observed, where grace is
called by the name of " spirit", it will appear that 'tis so called by
an ascription of the Holy Ghost, even the third person in the
Trinity, to that Divine principle in the hearts of the saints, as
though that principle in them were no other than the Spirit of God
itself, united to the soul, and living and acting in it, and exerting
itself in the use and improvement of its faculties.

Thus it is in the VIIIth chapter of Romans, as does manifestly
appear by verses 9-16—" But you are not in the flesh, but in the
Spirit, if so be the Spirit of God dwell in you," etc. " Now if
any man have not the Spirit of Christ, he is none of his," etc.

Here the apostle does fully explain himself what he means when he so often calls that holy principle that is in the hearts of the saints by the name "Spirit." This he means, the Spirit of God itself dwelling and acting in them. In the 9th verse he calls it the Spirit of God, and the Spirit of Christ in the 10th verse. He calls it Christ in them in the 11th verse. He calls it the Spirit of Him that raised up Jesus from the dead dwelling in them; and in the 14th verse he calls it the Spirit of God. In the 16th verse he calls it the Spirit itself. So it is called the Spirit of God in 1 Cor. ii. 11, 12. So that that holy, Divine principle, which we have observed does radically and essentially consist in Divine love, is no other than a communication and participation of that same infinite Divine love, which is GOD, and in which the God-head is eternally breathed forth; and subsists in the third person in the blessed Trinity. So that true saving grace is no other than that very love of God—that is, God, in one of the persons of the Trinity, uniting Himself to the soul of a creature, as a vital principle, dwelling there and exerting Himself by the faculties of the soul of man, in His own proper nature, after the manner of a principle of nature.

And we may look back and more fully understand what the apostle John means when he says once and again, " God is love," and " He that dwelleth in love dwelleth in God, and God in him," and " If we love one another, God dwelleth in us", and " His love is perfected in us", [and] " Hereby we know that we dwell in him and he is us, because he has given us of his Spirit."

By this, also, we may understand what the apostle Peter means in his 2d Epistle i. 4, that the saints are made " partakers of the divine nature." They are not only partakers of a nature that may, in some sense, be called Divine, because 'tis conformed to the nature of God; but the very deity does, in some sense, dwell in them. That holy and Divine love dwells in their hearts, and is so united to human faculties, that 'tis itself become a principle of new nature. That love, which is the very native tongue and spirit of God, so dwells in their souls that it exerts itself in its own nature in the exercise of those faculties, after the manner of a natural or vital principle in them.

This shews us how the saints are said to be the " temples of the Holy Ghost " as they are.

By this, also, we may understand how the saints are said to be made " partakers of God's holiness", not only as they partake of holiness that God gives, but partake of that holiness by which He himself is holy. For it has been already observed, the holiness of God consists in that Divine love in which the essence of God really flows out.

This also shews us how to understand our Lord when He speaks of His joy being fulfilled in the saints: John xvii. 13— ' And now come I to thee; and these things I speak in the world, that they might have my joy fulfilled in themselves." It is by the indwelling of that Divine Spirit, which we have shewn to be God the Father's and the Son's infinite love and joy in each other. In the 13th verse He says He has spoken His word to His disciples, " that his joy might be fulfilled; " and in verse 26th He says, " And I have declared unto them thy name, and will declare it; that the love wherewith thou hast loved me may be in them, and I in them."

And herein lies the mystery of the vital union that is between Christ and the soul of a believer, which orthodox divines speak so much of, Christ's love—that is, His Spirit is actually united to the faculties of their souls. So it properly lives, acts, and exerts its nature in the exercise of their faculties. By this Love being in them, He is in them, (John xvii. 26); and so it is said, 1 Cor. vi. 17—" But he that is joined unto the Lord is one spirit."

And thus it is that the saints are said to live, " yet not they, but Christ lives in them", (Gal. ii. 20). The very promise of spiritual life in their souls is no other than the Spirit of Christ himself. So that they live by His life, as much as the members of the body live by the life of the Lord, and as much as the branches live by the life of the root and stock. " Because I live, ye shall live also," (John xiv. 19). "Ye are dead: and your life is hid with Christ in God", (Col. iii. 3.) " When Christ, who is our life, shall appear," (Col. iii. 4.)

There is a union with Christ, by the indwelling of the love of Christ, two ways. First, as 'tis from Christ, and is the very Spirit and life and fulness of Christ; and second, as it acts to Christ. For the very nature of it is love and union of heart to Him.

Because the Spirit of God dwells as a vital principle or a principle of new life in the soul, therefore 'tis called the "Spirit of life," (Rom. viii. 2); and the Spirit that "quickens." (John vi. 63).

The Spirit of God is a vital principle in the soul, as the breath of life is in the body: Ezek. xxxvii. 5—"Thus saith the Lord God unto these bones, I will cause breath to enter into you, and ye shall live"; and so verses 9, 10. . . . .

That principle of grace that is in the hearts of the saints is as much a proper communication or participation of the Spirit of God, the third person in the Trinity, as that breath that entered into these bodies is represented to be a participation of the wind that blew upon them. The prophet says, "Come from the four winds, O breath, and breathe upon these slain that they may live," is now the very same wind and the same breath; but only was wanted to these bodies to be a vital principle in them, which otherwise would be dead. And therefore Christ himself represents the communication of His Spirit to His disciples by His breathing upon them, and communicating to them His breath, (John xx. 22).

We often, in our common language about things of this nature, speak of a principle of grace. I suppose there is no other principle of grace in the soul than the very Holy Ghost dwelling in the soul and acting there as a vital principle. To speak of a habit of grace as a natural disposition to act grace, as begotten in the soul by the first communication of Divine light, and as the natural and necessary consequence of the first light, it seems in some respects to carry a wrong idea with it. Indeed the first exercise of grace in the first light has a tendency to future acts, as from an abiding principle, by grace and by the covenant of God; but not by any natural force. The giving one gracious discovery or act of grace, or a thousand, has no proper natural tendency to cause an abiding habit of grace for the future; nor any otherwise than by Divine constitution and covenant. But all succeeding acts of grace must be as immediately, and, to all intents and purposes, as much from the immediate acting of the Spirit of God on the soul, as the first; and if God should take away His Spirit out of the soul, all habits and acts of grace would of themselves cease as immediately as light ceases in a room when a candle is carried out. And no man has a habit of grace dwelling in him any otherwise than as he has the Holy Spirit dwelling in him in his temple, and acting in union with his natural faculties, after the manner of a vital principle. So that when they act grace, 'tis, in the language of the apostle, " not they, but Christ living in them." Indeed the Spirit of God, united to human faculties, acts very much after the manner of a natural principle or habit. So that one act makes way for another, and so it now settles the soul in a disposition to holy acts; but that it does, so as by grace and covenant, and not from any natural necessity.

Hence the Spirit of God seems in sacred Scripture to be spoken of as a quality of the persons in whom it resided. So that they are called spiritual persons; as when we say a virtuous man, we speak of virtue as the quality of the man. 'Tis the Spirit itself that is the only principle of true virtue in the heart. So that to be truly virtuous is the same as to be spiritual.

And thus it is not only with respect to the virtue that is in the hearts of the saints on earth, but also the perfect virtue and holiness of the saints in heaven. It consists altogether in the indwelling and acting of the Spirit of God in their habits. And so it was with man before the Fall; and so it is with the elect, sinless angels. We have shewn that the holiness and happiness of God consist in the Holy Spirit; and so the holiness and happiness of every holy or truly virtuous creature of God, in heaven or earth, consist in the communion of the same Spirit.

OBSERVATIONS CONCERNING

THE SCRIPTURE OECONOMY OF THE TRINITY,

AND COVENANT OF REDEMPTION

WE should be careful that we do not go upon uncertain grounds, and fix uncertain determinations in things of so high a nature. The following things seem to be what we have pretty plain reason to determine with respect to those things.

1. That there is a subordination of the persons of the Trinity, in their actings with respect to the creature; that one acts from another, and under another, and with a dependance on another, in their actings, and particularly in what they act in the affairs of man's redemption. So that the Father in that affair acts as head of the Trinity, and the Son under Him, and the Holy Spirit under them both.

2. It is very manifest, that the persons of the Trinity are not inferiour one to another in glory and excellency of nature. The Son, for instance, is not inferiour to the Father in glory; for He is the brightness of His glory, the very image of the Father, the express and perfect image of His person. And therefore the Father's infinite happiness is in Him, and the way that the Father enjoys the glory of the deity is in enjoying Him. And though there be a priority of subsistence, and a kind of dependence of the Son, in His subsistence, on the Father; because with respect to His subsistence, He is wholly from the Father and is begotten by Him; yet this is more properly called priority than superiority, as we ordinarily use such terms. There is dependance without inferiority of deity; because in the Son the deity, the whole deity and glory of the Father, is as it were repeated or duplicated. Every thing in the Father is repeated, or expressed again, and that fully: so that there is properly no inferiority.

3. From hence it seems manifest, that the other persons' acting

under the Father does not arise from any natural subjection, as we should understand such an expression according to the common idiom of speech; for thus a natural subjection would be understood to imply either an obligation to compliance and conformity to another as a superiour and one more excellent, and so most worthy to be a rule for another to conform to; or an obligation to conformity to another's will, arising from a dependence on another's will for being or well-being. But neither of these can be the case with respect to the persons of the Trinity, for one is not superiour to another in excellency: neither is one in any respect dependant on another's will for being or well-being. For though one proceeds from another, and so may be said to be in some respects dependant on another, yet it is no dependance of one on the will of another. For it is no voluntary, but a necessary proceeding; and therefore infers no proper subjection of one to the will of another.

4. Though a subordination of the persons of the Trinity in their actings, be not from any proper natural subjection one to another, and so must be conceived of as in some respect established by mutual free agreement, whereby the persons of the Trinity, of their own will, have as it were formed themselves into a society, for carrying on the great design of glorifying the deity and communicating its fulness, in which is established a certain oeconomy and order of acting; yet this agreement establishing this oeconomy is not to be looked upon as meerly arbitrary, founded on nothing but the meer pleasure of the members of this society; nor meerly a determination and constitution of wisdom come into from a view to certain ends which it is very convenient for the obtaining. But there is a natural decency or fitness in that order and oeconomy that is established. It is fit that the order of the acting of the persons of the Trinity should be agreeable to the order of their subsisting. That as the Father is first in the order of subsisting, so He should be first in the order of acting. That as the other two persons are from the Father in their subsistence, and as to their subsistence naturally originated from Him and are dependant on Him; so that in all that they act they should

originate from Him, act from Him and in a dependance on Him. That as the Father with respect to the subsistences is the fountain of the deity, wholly and entirely so; so He should be the fountain in all the acts of the deity. This is fit and decent in itself. Though it is not proper to say, decency *obliges* the persons of the Trinity to come into this order and oeconomy; yet it may be said that decency requires it, and that therefore the persons of the Trinity all consent to this order, and establish it by agreement, as they all naturally delight in what is in itself fit, suitable and beautiful. Therefore,

5. This order or oeconomy of the persons of the Trinity with respect to their actions *ad extra*, is to be conceived of as prior to the covenant of redemption: as we must conceive of God's determination to glorify and communicate Himself as prior to the method that His wisdom pitches upon as tending best to effect this. For God's determining to glorify and communicate Himself must be conceived of as flowing from God's nature; or we must look upon God from the infinite fullness and goodness of His nature, as naturally disposed to cause the beams of His glory to shine forth, and His goodness to flow forth, yet we must look on the particular method that shall be chosen by divine wisdom to do this as not so directly and immediately owing to the natural disposition of the divine nature, as the determination of wisdom intervening, choosing the means of glorifying that disposition of nature. We must conceive of God's natural inclination as being exercised before wisdom is set to work to find out a particular excellent method to gratify that natural inclination. Therefore this particular invention of wisdom, of God's glorifying and communicating Himself by the redemption of a certain number of fallen inhabitants of this globe of earth, is a thing diverse from God's natural inclination to glorify and communicate Himself in general, and superadded to it or subservient to it. And therefore, that particular constitution or covenant among the persons of the Trinity about this particular affair, must be looked upon as in the order of nature after that disposition of the Godhead to glorify and communicate itself, and so

79

after the will of the persons of the Trinity to act, in so doing, in that order that is in itself fit and decent, and what the order of their subsisting requires. We must distinguish between the covenant of redemption, that is an establishment of wisdom wonderfully contriving a particular method for the most conveniently obtaining a great end, and that establishment that is founded in fitness and decency and the natural order of the eternal and necessary subsistence of the persons of the Trinity. And this must be conceived of as prior to the other.

It is evident by the Scripture, that there is an eternal covenant between some of the persons of the Trinity, about that particular affair of men's redemption; and therefore that some things that appertain to the particular office of some of the persons and their particular order and manner of acting in this affair, do result from a particular new agreement; and not meerly from the order already fixed in a preceding establishment founded in the nature of things, together with the new determination of redeeming mankind. There is something else new besides a new particular determination of a work to be done for God's glorying and communicating Himself. There is a particular covenant entered into about that very affair, settling something new concerning the part that some at least of the persons are to act in that affair.

6. That the oeconomy of the persons of the Trinity, establishing that order of their acting that is agreeable to the order of their subsisting, is entirely diverse from the covenant of redemption and prior to it, not only appears from the nature of things; but appears evidently from the Scripture, being plainly deduced from the following things evidently collected thence.

(1). It is the determination of God the Father, whether there shall be any such thing admitted as redemption of sinners. It is His law, majesty and authority, as supreme ruler, legislatour and judge, that is contemned.

He is every where represented as the person who, (in the place that He stands in among the persons of the Trinity), is especially injured by sin, and who is therefore the Person whose wrath is enkindled, and whose justice and vengeance are to be executed, and must be satisfied. And therefore, it is at His will and determination whether He will on any terms forgive sinners; and so whether there shall be any redemption of them allowed any more than of fallen angels. But we must conceive of the determination that a redemption shall be allowed for fallen men, as preceding the covenant or agreement of the persons of the Trinity relating to the particular manner and means of it; and consequently, that the Father, who determines whether a redemption shall be allowed or no, acts as the head of the society of the Trinity, and in the capacity of supreme Lord and one that sustains the dignity and maintains the rights of the Godhead antecedently to the covenant of redemption; and consequently, that that oeconomy by which He stands in this capacity is prior to that covenant.

(2). Nothing is more plain from Scripture than that the Father chooses the person that shall be the Redeemer, and appoints Him; and that the Son has His authority in His office wholly from Him: which makes it evident, that that oeconomy by which the Father is head of the Trinity, is prior to the covenant of redemption. For He acts as such in the very making of that covenant, in choosing the person of the Redeemer to be covenanted with about that work. The Father is the head of the Trinity, and is invested with a right to act as such, before the Son is invested with the office of a Mediator. Because the Father, in the exercise of His Headship, invests the Son with that office. By which it is evident, that that establishment, by which the Father is invested with His character as head of the Trinity, precedes that which invests the Son with His character of Mediator; and therefore precedes the covenant of redemption; which is the establishment that invests the Son with that character. If the Son were invested with the office of a Mediator by the same establishment and agreement of the persons of the Trinity by which the Father is invested with power to act as Head of the Trinity, then the Father could not be said to elect and appoint the Son to His office of Mediator, and invest Him with authority for it, any more than the Son elects and invests the Father with His character of Head of the

Trinity; or any more than the Holy Ghost elects both the Son
and the Father to their several oeconomical offices; and the Son
would receive His powers to be a mediator no more from the
Father, than from the Holy Ghost. Because in this scheme it
is supposed, that, prior to the covenant of redemption, all the
persons act as upon a level, and each Person, by one common
agreement in that covenant of redemption, is invested with His
proper office; the Father with that of Head, the Son with that of
Mediator, the Spirit with that of common emissary and con-
summatour of the designs of the other two. So that by this
supposition no one has His office by the particular appointment
of any one singly, or more than another; but all alike by common
consent; there being no antecedent establishment giving one any
power of headship over another, to authorize or appoint another.

(3). That the forementioned oeconomy of the persons of the
Trinity is diverse from all that is established in the covenant of
redemption and prior to it, is further confirmed by this, that
this oeconomy remains after the work of redemption is finished,
and every thing appertaining to it brought to its ultimate con-
summation, and the Redeemer shall present all that were to be
redeemed to the Father in perfect glory, having His work com-
pleatly finished upon them, and so shall resign up that dominion
that He received of the Father subservient to this work, agreeably
to what had been stipulated in the covenant of redemption. Then
the oeconomical order of the persons of the Trinity shall yet
remain, whereby the Father acts as Head of the society and
supreme Lord of all, and the Son and the Spirit [shall be][1] subject
unto Him. Yea, this oeconomical order shall not only remain,
but shall then and on that occasion become more visible and
conspicuous, and the establishment of things by the covenant of
redemption shall then, as it were, give place to this oeconomy
as prior; for thus the apostle represents the matter, 1 Cor. xv.
24–28. " Then cometh the end, when he shall have delivered up
the kingdom to God, even the Father; when he shall have put

[1] Words thus enclosed appear to be in the handwriting of Dr. Jonathan
Edwards, son of the first President.

down all rule and all authority and power. For he must reign till he has put all enemies under his feet. The last enemy that shall be destroyed is death. For he hath put all things under his feet. But when he saith, All things are put under him, it is manifest that he is excepted which did put all things under him. And when all things shall be subdued unto him, then shall the Son also himself be subject unto him that put all things under him, that God may be all in all."

Now if that establishment that settles the oeconomy of the persons of the Trinity, was no other than the covenant of redemption itself, or that agreement that the persons of the Trinity entered into establishing their order of acting in that affair, and assigning each one His part and office in that work; it would at least be unreasonable to suppose, that this oeconomy or order of the persons of the Trinity should be least conspicuous and manifest while this work lasts, and most so after the Redeemer has finished it and resigned His office; and that the resignation of His office should be to that end, that things might return to that oeconomical order, and be governed more conspicuously and manifestly agreeably to it.

(4). Another argument that shews the covenant of redemption to be entirely a distinct establishment from that which is the foundation of the oeconomy of the persons of the Trinity, is this, that the place and station that the Son attains to by this establishment is entirely distinct from that which He stands in by the oeconomy of the Trinity; insomuch that by the covenant of redemption the Son of God is for a season advanced into the oeconomical seat of another person, viz., of the Father; in being by this covenant established as the Lord and judge of the world, in the Father's stead and as His viceregent, and as ruling in the Father's throne, the throne that belongs to Him in His oeconomical station. For by the oeconomy of the Trinity it is the Father's province to act as the lawgiver and judge and disposer of the world.

(5). Another argument of the same thing is this, that the Scriptures do represent that the promises made to the Son in that covenent are made by the Father only, and that the honour and reward, that He has by that covenant, are granted only by the Father. Whereas, if the oeconomy empowring the Father thus to act as the Son's head, in making promises to Him and making over rewards to Him, were not prior to the covenant in which these promises are made and these things made over, the Father could have no power to make such promises, and grant such things to the Son: nor would it be done by the Father any more than by the Holy Spirit; for it would be done equally by all the persons of the Trinity acting conjunctly.

Concerning the COVENANT OF REDEMPTION. In order rightly to understand it and duly to distinguish it from the establishment of the oeconomy of the persons of the Trinity, the following things may be noted:

1. It is the Father that begins that great transaction of the eternal covenant of redemption, is the first mover in it, and acts in every respect as head in that affair. He determines to allow a redemption, and for whom it shall be. He pitches upon a person for a Redeemer. He proposes the matter unto Him, offers Him authority for the office, proposes precisely what He should do, as the terms of man's redemption, and all the work that He should perform in this affair, and the reward He should receive, and the success He should have. And herein the Father acts in the capacity in which He is already established; viz., that of head of the Trinity and all their concerns, and the fountain of all things that appertain to the deity, and its glorification and communication.

2. Though the Father, meerly by virtue of His oeconomical prerogative as head of the Trinity, is the first mover and beginner in the affair of our redemption, and determines that a redemption shall be admitted, and for whom, and proposes the matter first to His Son, and offers Him authority for the office; yet it is not meerly by virtue of His oeconomical prerogative, that He orders, determines and prescribes all that He does order and prescribe relating to it. But He does many things that He does in the work of redemption in the exercise of a new right, that He

84

acquires by a new establishment, a free covenant entered into between Him and His Son, in entering into which covenant the Son, (though He acts on the proposal of the Father), yet acts as one wholly in His own right, as much as the Father, being not under subjection or prescription in His consenting to what is proposed to Him, but acting as of Himself. Otherwise there would have been no need of the Father and Son's entering into covenant one with another, in order to the Son's coming into subjection and obligation to the Father, with respect to any thing appertaining to this affair. The whole tenour of the Gospel holds this forth, that the Son acts altogether freely and as [of] His own right, in undertaking the great and difficult and self-abasing work of our redemption, and that He becomes obliged to the Father with respect to it by voluntary covenant engagements, and not by any establishment prior thereto. So that He merits infinitely of the Father in entering into and fulfilling these engagements. The Father meerly by His oeconomical prerogative can direct and prescribe to the other persons of the Trinity in all things not below their oeconomical characters. But all those things that imply something below the infinite majesty and glory of divine persons, and which they cannot do, without, as it were, laying aside the divine glory, and stooping infinitely below the height of that glory; these things are below their oeconomical divine character; and therefore the Father cannot prescribe to the other persons any thing of this nature, without a new establishment by free covenant impowring Him so to do. But what is agreed for with the Son concerning His coming into the world in such a state of humiliation, and what He should do and suffer in that state, is His descending to a state infinitely below His divine dignity, and therefore the Father has no right to prescribe to Him with regard to those things, unless as invested with a right by free covenant engagements of His Son.

3. From what has been said it appears, that besides that oeconomical subordination of the persons of the Trinity that arises from the manner and order of their subsisting, there is a new kind of subordination and mutual obligation between two

of the persons, arising from this new establishment, the covenant of redemption, the Son undertaking and engaging to put Himself into a new kind of subjection to the Father, far below that of His oeconomical station, even the subjection of a proper servant to the Father, and one under His law, in the manner that creatures that are infinitely below God and absolutely dependant for their being on the meer will of God, are subject to His preceptive will and absolute legislative authority; engaging to become a creature, and so to put Himself in the proper circumstances of a servant: from which engagements of the Son the Father acquires a new right of headship and authority over the Son, to command Him and prescribe to Him and rule over Him, as His proper lawgiver and judge; and the Father, also, comes under new obligation to the Son, to give Him such success, rewards, etc.

4. It must be observed, that this subordination that two of the Persons of the Trinity come into, by the covenant of redemption, is not contrary to their oeconomical order; but in several respects agreeable to it, though it be new in kind. Thus, if either the Father or the Son be brought into the subjection of a servant to the other, it is much more agreeable to the oeconomy of the Trinity, that it should be the latter, who by that oeconomy is already under the Father as His head. That the Father should be servant to the Son would be contrary to the oeconomy and natural order of the persons of the Trinity.

5. It appears from what has been said, that no other subjection or obedience of the Son to the Father arises properly from the covenant of redemption, but only that which implies humiliation, or a state and relation to the Father wherein He descends below the infinite glory of a divine person: all that origination in acting from the Father, and dependance on and compliance with His will, that implies no descent below His divine glory, being no more than what properly flows from the oeconomical order of the persons of the Trinity. No other subjection or obedience is new in kind, but only that which implies humiliation; and if there were any such thing as a way of redemption without the humiliation of any divine person, the persons would act in man's

redemption in their proper subordination, without any covenant of redemption or any new establishment, as they do in the affair of rewarding the elect angels. It is true that if there were no humiliation of any divine person required, in order to man's redemption, the determination that there should be a redemption would be a determination not implied in the establishment of the oeconomy of the Trinity, as indeed the determination of no particular work is implied in that establishment. The establishment of the oeconomy is a determination that in whatever work is done, the persons shall act in such a subordination: but the determining what works shall be done is not implied in that establishment. God's determining to make a certain number of the angels happy to all eternity was not implied; but yet that being determined of the Father, the Son and the Spirit act in subordination to the Father in that affair of course, without any particular covenant or new establishment to settle the order of their acting in that particular affair. Meerly the work to be performed being superadded to the agreed general oeconomy, the order of their acting in that particular affair does [not] require any new agreement.

6. The obedience which the Son of God performs to the Father even in the affair of man's redemption, or as redeemer or mediator, before His humiliation, and also that obedience He performs as God-man after His humiliation, when as God-man He is exalted to the glory He had before, is no more than flows from His oeconomical office or character, although it be occasioned by the determination or decree of the work of redemption, which is something new, yea, is occasioned by the covenant of redemption. Yet that decree and covenant being supposed, such an obedience as He performs in His divine glory follows of course from His oeconomical character and station. Nor is it any other kind of obedience than what that character requires. There is no humiliation in it, and no part of it implies that new sort of subjection, that is engaged in the covenant of redemption.

7. Hence it comes to pass, that that obedience, that Christ performs to the Father even as mediator, and in the work of our

redemption, before His humiliation, and now, in His exalted state in heaven, is no part of that obedience that merits for sinners. For it is only that obedience which the Son voluntarily and freely subjected Himself to from love to sinners, and engaged to perform for them in the covenant of redemption, and that otherwise would not have belonged to Him, that merits for sinners. And that is only that obedience that implies an humiliation below His proper divine glory. Therefore it is only that obedience that He performs as made under the law, and in the form of a servant, that merits for us. The obedience He performs in the affair of our redemption in His state of exaltation does not merit for sinners, and is no more imputed to them than the obedience of the Holy Spirit.

8. As there is a kind of subjection, that the Son came into by the covenant of redemption, that does not belong to Him in His oeconomical character; which subjection He promises to the Father in that covenant: so also there is a kind of rule and authority which He receives by the covenant of redemption, which the Father promises Him, that does not belong to Him in His oeconomical character; viz. that of head of authority and rule to the universe, as Lord and judge of all. This does not belong to the Son but the Father by the oeconomy of the Trinity. It is the Father that is oeconomically the king of heaven and earth, lawgiver and judge of all. Therefore when the Son is made so, He is by the Father advanced into His throne, by having the Father's authority committed unto Him, to rule in His name and as His vicegerent. This the Father promised Him in the covenant of redemption as a reward for the forementioned subjection and obedience that He engaged in that covenant. And to put Him under greater advantages to obtain the success of His labours and sufferings in the work of redemption, this vicarious dominion of the Son is to continue to the end of the world; when the work of redemption will be finished, and the ends of the covenant of redemption obtained; when things will return ot be administered by the Trinity only, according to their oeconomical order.

9. Not only does the Son, by virtue of the covenant of

redemption, receive a new dignity of station which does not belong to Him meerly by the oeconomy of the Trinity, in the dominion he receives of the Father over the universe; but also in His having the dispensation and disposal of the Holy Spirit committed to Him. For when God exalted Jesus Christ, God-man, and set Him at His own right hand in heavenly places, and solemnly invested Him with the rule over the angels and over the whole universe; at the same time did He also give Him the great and main thing that He purchased, even the Holy Spirit, that He might have the disposal and dispensation of that, to the same purposes for which He had the government of the universe committed to Him, viz., to promote the grand designs of His redemption. (This is very evident by the Scripture). And this was a much greater thing, than God's giving Him the angels and the whole creation. For whereby the Father did, as it were, commit to Him His own divine infinite treasure, to dispense of it as He pleased to the redeemed, He made Him Lord of His house, and Lord of His treasures. This new authority that the Son receives with regard to the Spirit of God, at His enthronization at the Father's right hand, will be resigned at the end of the world, in like manner as He will then resign the new dominion that He then is invested with over the universe.

10. But it is to be observed, that there is a two-fold subjecting of the Holy Spirit to the Son, as our Redeemer, in some respect new and diverse from what is meerly by the oeconomy of the Trinity.

First. The Spirit is put under the Son, or given to Him and committed to His disposal and dispensation, as the Father's vicegerent and as ruling on His Father's throne; as the angels and the whole universe were given to Him to dispose of as the Father's vicegerent. So that the Holy Spirit, 'till the work of redemption shall be finished, will continue to act under the Son, in some respects, with that subjection that is oeconomically due to the Father. For the Son will have the disposal of the Spirit in the name of the Father, or as ruling with His authority. This authority that the Son has over the Spirit, will be resigned at the end of the world, when He shall resign His vicarious dominion and authority, that God may be all in all, and that things thenceforward may be dispensed only according to the order of the oeconomy of the Trinity.

Secondly. There is another subjecting of the Spirit to the Son, that is in some respect diverse from what is meerly by the oeconomy of the Trinity, and that is, a giving Him to Him not as the Father's vicegerent, but only as God-man and husband, and vital head of the Church. All that is new in this subjection is this, that, whereas by the oeconomy of the Trinity the Spirit acts under the Son as God or a divine person, He now acts in like manner under the same person in two natures united, or as God-man, and in His two natures the husband and vital head of the Church. This subjection of the Spirit to Christ will continue to eternity, and never will be resigned up. For Christ, God-man, will continue to all eternity to be the vital head and husband of the Church, and the vital good, that this vital head will eternally communicate to His church, will be the Holy Spirit. The Spirit was the inheritance that Christ, as God-man, purchased for Himself and His church, or for Christ mystical; and it was the inheritance that He, as God-man, received of the Father, at His ascension, for Himself and them. But the inheritance He purchased and received, is an eternal inheritance. It is, in this regard, with the authority with which Christ was invested at His ascension, with respect to the Spirit, as it is with the authority which He then received over the world. He then was invested with a two-fold dominion over the world, one, vicarious, or as the Father's vicegerent, which shall be resigned at the end of the world: the other, as Christ, God-man and head and husband of the Church, and in this latter respect He will never resign His dominion, but will reign forever and ever, as is said of the saints in the new-Jerusalem, after the end of the world, Rev. xxii. 5.

11. Though the subjection of the Holy Spirit to the Son has, in these respects that have been mentioned, something in it that is new and diverse from that subjection that flows meerly from

the oeconomical order of the Persons; yet it is only circumstancially new; it is not new in that sense, as to be properly a new kind of subjection, as the Son's subjection to the Father as made under the law is. There is no humiliation or abasement in this new subjection of the Spirit to the Son. The Spirit's subjection to the Son as God-man, (though the human nature in its union with the divine be a sharer with the divine in this honour and authority), implies no abasement of the Spirit; i.e., is no lower sort of subjection, than that which the Holy Spirit is in to the Son by the oeconomy of the Trinity. When once the eternal Son of God was become man, and this person was not only God, but God-man, this person considered as God-man was a no less honourable person than [He][1] was before: and especially was it visibly and conspicuously so, when this complex person was exalted by the Father to His throne, for God the Father glorified Him as God-man, with the glory that He had before the world was. And therefore, divine respect was as properly due to Him as before; and the respect, that was before due to the second person by the oeconomy of the Trinity, is now given to Him by all, without any abasement of those that give it. It is given by angels and men without any debasing or degrading of their worship. And the same subjection is yielded by the Holy Spirit that it before yielded according to the oeconomy of the persons, without stooping at all below the station the Spirit stood in with respect to the Son before. And when once it has pleased the Father to set the Son on His throne, as His vicegerent, the subjection of the Spirit to the Son, as to the Father, follows of course, without any stooping below the dignity of His oeconomical character. The Holy Spirit is not thus subject to the Son by any abasement He submits to, by any special covenant; but by the gift of the Father, exercising His prerogative as Head of the Trinity, as He is by His oeconomical character.

12. From what has been now observed, we may learn the reason why the obedience of the Holy Spirit to the Son, though it be in some respect new, and for our sakes, yet is not meritorious

[1] For 'it', as written by the copyist.

for us; viz., that it implies no humiliation, is properly no new kind of subjection or obedience besides what, under such circumstances, flows from the oeconomical order of the persons of the Trinity. As I observed before, it is only that obedience of the Son of God that merits for sinners, that is properly new in kind, and implies humiliation. Hence the Scripture mentions no reward that the Holy Spirit receives of His obedience for us or Himself.

13. The things that have been observed, naturally lead us to suppose, that the covenant of redemption is only between two of the persons of the Trinity; viz., the Father and the Son. For, as has been observed, there is need of a new establishment, or particular covenant, only on account of the new kind of subjection of the Son, and the humiliation He is the subject of in His office of Mediator, wherein He stoops below His proper oeconomical character. Otherwise, there would be no more need of a new establishment, by a special covenant in this affair, than concerning God's dealing with the elect angels, or any other work of God whatsoever. But it is the Son only that is made the subject of this humiliation: which humiliation was in His new subjection and obedience to the Father. Therefore the covenant of redemption is only between the Father and the Son. Neither is there any intimation in Scripture of any such thing as any covenant, either of the Father, or the Son, with the Holy Ghost. He is never represented as a party in this covenant, but the Father and the Son only. The covenant of redemption, which is the new covenant, the covenant with the second Adam, that which takes effect in the second place, (though entered into first in order of time), after the covenant with the first Adam was broken, was made only between God the lawgiver, and man's surety and representative; as the first covenant, that was made with the first Adam, was. The covenant of redemption was the covenant in which God the Father made over an eternal reward to Christ mystical, and therefore was made only with Christ the head of that body. No proper reward was promised or made over in that covenant to the Holy Ghost, although the end of it was the honour and glory of all the persons of the Trinity.

14. It is true, that the Holy Spirit is infinitely concerned in the affair of our redemption, as well as the Father and the Son, and equally with them; and therefore we may well suppose, that the affair was, as it were, concerted among all the persons, and determined by the perfect consent of all. And that there was a consultation among the three persons about it, as much doubtless as about the creating of man, (for the work of redemption is a work wherein the distinct concern of each person is infinitely greater, than in the work of creation), and so, that there was a joint agreement of all; but not properly a covenant between them all. There is no necessity of supposing, that each one acts, in this consent and agreement, as a party covenanting; or that the agreement of each one is of the nature of a covenant, stipulation and engagement.

15. It is not only true, that the Holy Ghost is concerned in the *work of redemption* equally with the other persons; but that He is also concerned in the *covenant of redemption*, as well as they. And His concern in this covenant is as great as theirs, and equally honourable with theirs, and yet His concern in the covenant is not that of a party covenanting.

COROL. From the things that have been observed, it appears to be unreasonable to suppose, as some do, that the SONSHIP of the second person in the Trinity consists only *in the relation He bears to the Father in His mediatorial character;* and that His generation or proceeding from the Father *as a Son,* consists only in His being appointed, constituted and authorized of the Father to the office of a mediator; and that there is no other priority of the Father to the Son but that which is voluntarily established in the covenant of redemption. For it appears by what has been said, that the priority of the Father to the Son is, in the order of nature, before the covenant of redemption. And it appears evidently to be so, even by the scheme of those now mentioned, who suppose the contrary. For they suppose that it is the Father who by His power constitutes the Son in His office of mediator, and so that the mediator is His Son, *i.e.,* is made a mediator by Him, deriving His being in that office wholly from Him. But if so, that supposes the Father, in the oeconomy of the Trinity, to be before the Son or above Him (and so to vest with authority and thus to constitute and authorize the other person in the Trinity) before that other person is thus authorized, which is by the covenant of redemption, and consequently that this superiority of the Father is antecedent to that covenant. And the whole tenour of the gospel exhibits the same thing. For that represents the wondrous love and grace of God as appearing in appointing and constituting His own only begotten and beloved Son, to be our mediator; which would be absurd, if He were not *God's Son*, till after He was appointed to be our mediator.[1]

[1] This interpretation of Christ's Sonship was offered by Thomas Ridgley in his *Body of Divinity* (1731).—H.

APPENDIX[1]

" Many difficulties used to arise in my mind about our being saved upon the account of faith, as being the *condition* upon which God has promised salvation; as being that particular grace and virtue for which men are saved. According to which there is no difference between the condition of the first covenant and the second, but this: before the fall, man was to be saved upon the account of all the virtues; and since, upon the account only of one virtue and grace, even this of faith; for where is the difference? . . .

" But it seems to me that all this confusion arises from the wrong distinction men make between the covenant of grace and the covenant of redemption. It seems to me to be true, that as this first covenant was made with the first Adam, so the second covenant was made with the second Adam. As the first covenant was made with the seed of the first Adam no otherwise than as it was with them in him, so the second covenant is not made with the seed of the second Adam any otherwise than as it was·made with them in Him. . . . As the condition of the first covenant was Adam's standing, so the condition of the second covenant is Christ's standing. Christ has performed the condition of the new covenant. . . . We can do nothing but only receive Christ and what He has done already. Salvation is not offered to us upon any condition, but freely and for nothing. We are to do nothing for it; we are only to take it. This *taking* and *receiving* is *faith*. It is not said, If you will do so, you may have salvation; you may have the water of life; but, Come and take it; whosoever will, let him come. It is very improper to say that a *covenant* is made with men, any otherwise than in Christ; for there is a vast difference between a free offer and a covenant. The covenant was made with Christ, and in Him with His mystical body; and the condition of the covenant is Christ's perfect obedience

---

[1] The connecting notes in the Appendix are those of the original editor E. C. Smythe.—H.

95

and sufferings. And that, that is made to men, is a free *offer*. That, which is commonly called the *covenant of grace*, is only *Christ's open and free offer of life*, whereby He holds it out in His hand to sinners, and offers it without any condition. Faith cannot be called the *condition* of receiving, for it is the *receiving* itself; Christ holds out, and believers receive. There was no covenant made or agreement, upon something that must be done before they might receive. It is true, those that do not believe are not saved, and all that do believe are saved; that is, all that do receive Christ and salvation, they receive it, and all that will not receive salvation never do receive it, and never have it. But faith, or the reception of it, is not the *condition* of receiving it. It is not proper when a man holds out his gift to a beggar, that he may take it without any manner of preliminary conditions, to say that he makes a covenant with the beggar. No more proper is it to say, that Christ's holding forth life in His hand to us, that we may receive it, is making a covenant with us. But, I must confess, after all, that if men will call this free offer and exhibition a covenant, they may; and if they will call the *receiving* of life the condition of receiving of life, they are at liberty so to do; but I believe it is much the more hard for them to think right, for speaking so wrong.

"This making faith a *condition* of life fills the mind with innumerable difficulties about faith and works, and how to distinguish them. It tends to make us apt to depend on our own righteousness. It tends to lead men into Neonomianism, and gives the principal force to their arguments; whereas, if we would leave off distinguishing the covenant of grace and the covenant of redemption, we should have all those matters plain and unperplexed."

Much later, in another essay, he treats of the two covenants of grace and redemption, as follows,—not so much changing his ground, as finding room for the former by precise definition:—

"It seems to me, there arises considerable confusion from not rightly distinguishing between the covenant that God made with Christ and with His church or believers in Him, and the covenant between Christ and His church, or between Christ and men. There is doubtless a difference between the covenant that God makes with Christ and His people, considered as one, and the covenant of Christ and His people between themselves. The covenant that a father makes with his son and his son's wife, considered as one, must be looked upon as different from the marriage covenant, or the covenant which the son and the wife make between themselves. The father is concerned in this covenant only as a parent in a child's marriage, directing, consenting, and ratifying. These covenants are often confounded, and the promises of each are called the promises of the covenant of grace, without due distinction. Which has perhaps been the occasion of many difficulties, and considerable confusion in discourses and controversies about the covenant of grace. . . .

" These covenants differ in their conditions. The condition of the covenant that God has made with Jesus Christ, as a public person, is *all that Christ has done and suffered to procure redemption.* The condition of Christ's covenant with His people, or of the marriage covenant between Him and men, is *that they should close with Him and adhere to Him.* They also differ in their promises. The sum of what is promised by the Father, in the former of these covenants, is Christ's reward for what He has done in the work of redemption, and success therein. And the sum of what is promised in Christ's marriage covenant with His people, is the enjoyment of Himself, and communion with Him in the benefits He Himself has obtained of the Father by what He has done and suffered; as in marriage the persons covenanting give themselves and all that they have to each other."

Again, in a subsequent paper:—

" There are two covenants that are made, that are by no means to be confounded one with another: 1. The covenant of God the Father with the Son, and with all the elect in Him, whereby things are said to be given in Christ before the world began, and to be promised before the world began. . . . 2. There is another covenant, that is the marriage covenant between Christ and the soul; the covenant of union, or whereby the soul becomes united to Christ. This covenant before marriage is only an offer or invitation: ' Behold, I stand at the door and knock,' etc. In marriage, or in the soul's conversion, it becomes a proper covenant. This is what is called the *covenant of grace*, in distinction from the covenant of *redemption*."

Later still he elaborates and confirms the same distinctions, and adds:—

" The due consideration of these things may perhaps reconcile the difference between those divines that think the covenant of redemption and the covenant of grace the same, and those that think them different. The covenant that God the Father makes with believers is indeed the very same with the covenant of redemption made with Christ before the foundation of the world, or at least is entirely included in it. And this covenant has a mediator, or is ordained in the hand of a mediator. But the covenant, by which Christ Himself and believers are united one with another, is properly a different covenant from that; and is not made by a mediator. There is a mediator between sinners and the Father, to bring about a covenant union between them; but there is no mediator between Christ and sinners, to bring about a marriage union between Christ and their souls.

" These things may also tend to reconcile the difference between those divines that think the covenant of grace is not conditional as to us, or that the promises of it are without any proper conditions to be performed by us; and those that think that faith is the proper condition of the covenant of grace. The covenant of grace, if hereby we understand the covenant between God the Father and believers in Christ, . . . is indeed without any proper conditions to be performed by us. Faith is not properly the condition of the covenant, but the righteousness of Christ. . . . But the covenant of grace, if thereby we understand the covenant between Christ Himself and His church as His members, is conditional as to us. The proper condition of it, which is a yielding to Christ's invitations, and accepting His offers, and closing with Him as a redeemer and spiritual husband, is to be performed by us."

AN ESSAY ON THE TRINITY [1]

Tɪs common when speaking of the divine happiness to say that
God is infinitely happy in the enjoyment of Himself, in perfectly
beholding and infinitely loving, and rejoicing in, His own essence
and perfections, and accordingly it must be supposed that God
perpetually and eternally has a most perfect idea of Himself, as it
were an exact image and representation of Himself ever before
Him and in actual view, and from hence arises a most pure and
perfect act or energy in the Godhead, which is the Divine love,
complacence and joy.

   Tho' we cannot conceive of the manner of the Divine understanding, yet if it be understanding or any thing that can be any
way signified by that word of ours, it is by idea.   Tho the Divine
nature be vastly different from that of created spirits, yet our
souls are made in the image of God, we have understanding and
will, idea and love as God hath, and the difference is only in the
perfection of degree and manner.   The perfection of the manner
will indeed infer this that there is no distinction to be made in
God between power and habit and act, and with respect to God's
understanding that there are no such distinctions to be admitted
as in ours between perception or idea, and reasoning and judgment, (excepting what the will has to do in judgment), but that
the whole of the Divine understanding or wisdom consists in the
meer perception or unvaried presence of His infinitely perfect
idea, and with respect to the other faculty as it is in God there
are no distinctions to be admitted of faculty, habit, and act,
between will, inclination, and love, but that it is all one simple
act.   But the Divine perfection will not infer [*i.e.,* imply] that

<hr>

   [1] The Essay is printed from a careful transcription of the original. It is given in
the unrevised form in which it was left by the author, with no attempt to mend
the orthography or the structure of the sentences. The alterations are few and
trifling in their nature, being designed exclusively to remove obscurities as to
the meaning which might perplex the reader. I have thought it better to err by
too slight changes than in the opposite direction.

His understanding is not by idea and that there is not indeed such a thing as inclination and love in God.[1]

[That in John   God is love shews that there are more persons than one in the deity, for it shews love to be essential and necessary to the deity so that His nature consists in it, and this supposes that there is an eternal and necessary object, because all love respects another that is the beloved. By love here the apostle certainly means something beside that which is commonly called self-love: that is very improperly called love and is a thing of an exceeding diverse nature from the affection or virtue of love the apostle is speaking of.]

The sum of the Divine understanding and wisdom consists in His having a perfect idea of Himself, He being indeed the all: the all-comprehending being,—He that is, and there is none else. So the sum of His inclination, love, and joy is His love to and delight in Himself. God's love to Himself, and complacency and delight in Himself,—they are not to be distinguished, they are the very same thing in God; which will easily be allowed, love in man being scarcely distinguishable from the complacence he has in any idea: if there be any difference it is meerly modal, and circumstantial.

The knowledge or view which God has of Himself must necessarily be conceived to be some thing distinct from His meer direct existence. There must be something that answers to our reflection. The reflection as we reflect on our own minds carries some thing of imperfection in it. However, if God beholds Himself so as thence to have delight and joy in Himself He must become His own object. There must be a duplicity. There is God and the idea of God, if it be proper to call a conception of that that is purely spiritual an idea.

And I do suppose the deity to be truly and properly repeated by God's thus having an idea of Himself and that this idea of God is truly God,[2] to all intents and purposes, and that by this means the Godhead is really generated and repeated.

[1] The next paragraph is inserted at a later date.
[2] Over the last three words is written, as an alternate reading, 'is a substantial idea and has the very essence of God'.

1.   God's idea of Himself is absolutely perfect and therefore is an express and perfect image of Him, exactly like Him in every respect; there is nothing in the pattern but what is in the representation,—substance, life, power nor any thing else, and that in a most absolute perfection of similitude, otherwise it is not a perfect idea.   But that which is the express, perfect image of God and in every respect like Him is God to all intents and purposes, because there is nothing wanting: there is nothing in the deity that renders it the deity but what has some thing exactly answering it in this image, which will therefore also render that the deity.

2.   But this will more clearly appear if we consider the nature of spiritual ideas or ideas of things purely spiritual, these that we call ideas of reflection, such as our ideas of thought, love, fear, etc. If we diligently attend to them we shall find they are repetitions of these very things either more fully or faintly, or else they are only ideas of some external circumstances that attend them, with a supposition of something *like* what we have in our minds, that is, attended with like circumstances.   Thus 'tis easy to perceive that if we have an idea of thought 'tis only a repetition of the same thought with the attention of the mind to that repetition.   So if we think of love either of our [illegible] love or of the love of others that we have not, we either so frame things in our imagination that we have for a moment a love to that thing or to something we make to represent it and stand for it, or we excite for a moment the love that we have to something else and suppose something like it there, or we only have an idea of the name with some of the concomitants and effects and suppose something unseen that [is] used to be signified by that name.   And such kind of ideas very commonly serve us, tho they are not indeed real ideas of the thing it self.   But we have learn'd by experience and it has become habitual to us to govern our thoughts, judgment and actions about it as tho' we conceived of the thing it self.   But if a person has truly and properly an idea of any act of love, of fear or anger or any other act or motion of the mind, things must be ordered and framed in his mind that

he must for that moment have something of a consciousness of
the same motions either to the same thing, or to something else
that is made to represent it in the mind, or towards something
else that is pro re nata thither referd and as it were transposed,
and this consciousness of the same motions, with a design to
represent the other by them, is the idea it self we have of them,
and if it be perfectly clear and full it will be in all respects the very
same act of mind of which it is the idea, with this only difference
that the being of the latter is to represent the former.[1]

[If a man could have an absolutely perfect idea of all that pass'd
in his mind, all the series of ideas and exercises in every respect
perfect as to order, degree, circumstance etc. for any particular
space of time past, suppose the last hour, he would really to all
intents and purpose be over again what he was that last hour.
And if it were possible for a man by reflection perfectly to contemplate all that is in his own mind in an hour, as it is and at the
same time that it is there in its first and direct existence; if a man,
that is, had a perfect reflex or contemplative idea of every thought
at the same moment or moments that that thought was and of
every exercise at and during the same time that that exercise was,
and so through a whole hour, a man would really be two during
that time, he would be indeed double, he would be twice at once.
The idea he has of himself would be himself again.

Note, by having a reflex or contemplative idea of what passes
in our own minds I don't mean consciousness only. There is
a great difference between a man's having a view of himself,
reflex or contemplative idea of himself so as to delight in his own
beauty or excellency, and a meer direct consciousness. Or if we
mean by consciousness of what is in our own minds any thing
besides the meer simple existence in our minds of what is there,
it is nothing but a power by reflection to view or contemplate
what passes.

But the foregoing position, about a man's being twofold or
twice at once, is most evident by what has been said of the nature
of spiritual ideas, for every thing that a man is in that hour he

---

[1] The next three paragraphs were inserted at a later date.

is twice fully and perfectly. For all the ideas or thoughts that he has are twice perfectly and every judgmt [judgment] made and every exercise of inclination or affection, every act of the mind.]

Therefore as God with perfect clearness, fullness and strength, understands Himself, views His own essence (in which there is no distinction of substance and act but which is wholly substance and wholly act), that idea which God hath of Himself is absolutely Himself. This representation of the Divine nature and essence is the Divine nature and essence again: so that by God's thinking of the deity must certainly be generated. Hereby there is another person begotten, there is another infinite eternal almighty and most holy and the same God, the very same divine nature.

And this person is the second person in the Trinity, the only begotten and dearly beloved Son of God; He is the eternal, necessary, perfect, substantial and personal idea which God hath of Himself; and that it is so seems to me to be abundantly confirmed by the word of God.

1. Nothing can more agree with the account the Scripture gives us of the Son of God, His being in the form of God and His express and perfect image and representation: 2 Cor. iv. 4,—" lest the light of the glorious gospel of Christ who is the image of God, should shine unto them." Philip. ii. 6—" Who being in the form of God." Colos. i. 15—"Who is the image of the invisible God." Heb. i. 3,—" Who being the brightness of his glory, and the express image of his person."[1] [In the original it is χαρακτὴρ τῆς ὑποστάσεως αὐτοῦ which denotes one person as like another as the impression on the wax is to the engraving on the seal. (Hurrion, " of Christ Crucified," vol. 1, p. 189, 190)[2]; and what can more agree with this that I suppose, that the Son of God is the divine idea of Himself.] What [can] be more properly called the image of a thing than the idea. The end of other

---

[1] What next follows, within brackets, is a later insertion.
[2] John Hurrion (1675?–1731) was an English Independent divine. *The Knowledge of Christ and Him Crucified . . . applied in eight sermons* was published in 1727.—H.

images is to beget an idea of the things they represent in us, but the idea is the most immediate representation, and seems therefore to be a more primary sort of image, and we know of no other spiritual images nor images of spiritual things but ideas. An idea of a thing seems more properly to be called an image or representation of that thing than any distinct being can be. However exactly one being—suppose one human body—be like another, yet I think one is not in the most proper sense the image of the other but more properly in the image of the other. Adam did not beget a son that was his image properly, but in his image; but the Son of God—He is not only in the image of the Father, but He is the image itself in the most proper sense. The design of an idea is to represent, and the very being of an idea consists in similitude and representation: if it don't actually represent to the beholder, it ceases to be. And the being of it is immediately dependent on its pattern: its reference to that ceasing, it ceases to be its idea.

That Christ is this most immediate representation of the Godhead, viz. the idea of God, is in my apprehension confirmed by John. xii. 45—"He that seeth me seeth him that sent me", and John. xiv. 7, 8, 9—"If ye had known me, ye should have known my Father also: and from henceforth ye know him, and have seen him. Philip saith unto him, Lord shew us the Father, and it sufficeth us. Jesus saith unto him, Have I been so long time with you, and yet hast thou not known me Philip? he that hath seen me hath seen the Father and how sayest thou then, Shew us the Father?" See also John xv. 22, 23, 24. Seeing the perfect idea of a thing is to all intents and purposes the same as seeing the thing: it is not only equivalent to the seeing of it but it is the seeing it: for there is no other seeing but having the idea. Now by seeing a perfect idea, so far as we see it, we have it. But it can't be said of any thing else that in the seeing of it we see another, strictly speaking, except it be the very idea of the other.

2. This well agrees with what the Scriptures teach us ever was God's love to and delight in His Son. For the idea of God is that image of God that is the object of God's eternal and infinite

love and in which He hath perfect joy and happiness. God undoubtedly infinitely loves and delights in Himself and is infinitely
happy in the understanding and view of His own glorious
essence: this is commonly said. The same the Scripture teaches
us concerning that image of God that is His Son. The Son of
God—He is the true David or beloved. John. iii. 35 and v. 20.
The Father loveth the Son. So it was declared at Christ's baptism
and transfiguration, this is my beloved Son in whom I am well
pleased. So the Father calls Him His elect in whom His soul delighteth. The infinite happiness of the Father consists in the
enjoymt. of His Son: Prov. viii, 30, I was daily His delight *i.e.*
before the world was. It seems to me most probable that God
has His infinite happiness but one way, and that the infinite joy
He has in His own idea and that which He has in his Son are but
one and the same.

3. Christ is called the face of God, Exod. xxxiii. 14: the word
in the original signifies face, looks, form or appearance. Now
what can be so properly and fitly called so with respect to God as
God's own perfect idea of Himself whereby He has every moment
a view of His own essence: this idea is that face of God which
God sees as a man sees his own face in a looking glass. 'Tis of
such form or appearance whereby God eternally appears to Himself. The root that the original word comes from signifies to
look upon or behold: now what is that which God looks upon
or beholds in so emminent a manner as He doth on His own
idea or that perfect image of Himself which He has in view. This
is what is eminently in God's presence and is therefore called the
angel of God's presence or face. Isia. lxiii. 9.

4. This seems also well to agree with Christ being called the
brightness, effulgence or shining forth of God's glory upon two
accounts: 1, because 'tis by God's idea that His Glory shines forth
and appears to Himself. God may be conceived of as glorious
antecedent to His idea of Himself, but then his glory is latent;
but 'tis the idea by which it shines forth and appears to God's view
so that he can delight in it. 2. God is well represented by the
luminary and His idea by the light, for what is so properly the

light of a mind or spirit as its knowledge or understanding? The understanding or knowledge of God is much more properly represented by light in a luminary than the understanding of a created mind, for knowledge is light rather let into a created mind than shining from it, but the understanding of the Divine mind originally proceeds from this mind it self and derived from no other.

5. But that the Son of God is God's own eternal and perfect idea is a thing we have yet much more expressly revealed in God's word. First, in that Christ is called the wisdom of God. If we are taught in the Scripture that Christ is the same with God's wisdom or knowledge, then it teaches us that He is the same with God's perfect and eternal idea. They are the same as we have already observed and I suppose none will deny. But Christ is said to be the wisdom of God: 1 Cor. i. 24, Luke xi, 49, compare with Matt. xxiii. 34; and how much doth Christ speak in Prov. under the name of wisdom especially in the viii. chap. We there have wisdom thus declaring, 22 verse, "The LORD possessed me in the beginning of his way, before his works of old. I was set up from ever-lasting . . . or ever the earth was. When there were no depths, I was brought forth; when there were no fountains abounding with water. Before the mountains were settled, before the hills was I brought forth: while as yet he had not made the earth nor the fields, nor the highest part of the dust of the world. When he prepared the heavens, I was there: when he set a compass upon the face of the depth: when he established the clouds," etc. 30 verse. "Then I was by him as one brought up with him: and I was daily his delight, rejoicing always before him; rejoicing in the habitable part of his earth; and my delights were with the sons of men." It has been usual to say that he that God possessed and set up from everlasting and that was brought forth before the world was, that was by God as His companion and as one brought up with Him, that was daily His delight, was the personal wisdom of God and if so it was God's personal idea of Himself.

Secondly, in That the Scripture teaches us that Christ is the logos of God. It will appear that this logos is the same with the idea of God, whether we interpret it of the reason of God or the word of God. If it signifies the reason and understanding of God, I suppose it won't be denied that 'tis the same thing with God's idea. If we translate it the word of God, He is either the outward word of God, or His inward. None will say He is His outward. Now the outward word is speech whereby ideas are outwardly expressed. The inward word is thought or idea it self. The Scripture being its own interpreter see how often is thinking in Scripture called saying or speaking, when applied to both God and men. The inward word is the pattern or original of which the outward word by which God has revealed himself is the copy. Now that which is the original from whence the revelation which God hath made of Himself is taken and the pattern to which it is conformed, is God's idea of Himself. When God declares Himself it is doubtless from and according to the idea He hath of Himself.

Thirdly, to the same purpose is another name by which Christ is called, viz. the AMEN, which is a Hebrew word that signifies truth. Now what is that which is the prime, original and universal truth but that which is in the Divine mind, viz. His eternal or infinite knowledge or idea.

And joining this with what was observed before, I think we may be bold to say that that which is the form, face and express and perfect image of God, in beholding which is His eternal delight, and is also the wisdom and knowledge, logos and truth of God, is God's idea of Himself. What other knowledge of God is there that is the form, appearance and perfect image and representation of God but God's idea of Himself.

And how well doth this agree with His office of being the great prophet and teacher of mankind, the light of the world and the revealer of God to creatures: John viii. 12—" I am the light of the world." Math. xi. 27—"No man knoweth the Father save the Son and He to whomsoever the Son will reveal him." John. i. 18 —" No man hath seen God at any time, the only begotten Son which is in the bosom of the Father, he hath declared him." Who can be so properly appointed to be revealer of God to the

JONATHAN EDWARDS

world as that person who is God's own perfect idea or understanding of Himself. Who can be so properly generated to be
the light by which God's glory shall appear to creatures, as He is
[—]that effulgence of His glory by which He appears to Himself.
And this is intimated to us in the Scriptures to be the reason why
Christ is the light of the world and the revealer of God to men
because He is the image of God, 2 Cor. iv. 4, lest the
light of the glorious gospel of Christ, who is the image of God,
should shine unto them." Joh. xii. 45, 46, "And he that seeth
me seeth him that sent me. I am come a light into the world,
that whosoever believeth on me should not abide in darkness."

The Godhead being thus begotten by God's loving an idea of
Himself and shewing forth in a distinct subsistence or person in
that idea, there proceeds a most pure act, and an infinitely holy
and sacred energy arises between the Father and Son in mutually
loving and delighting in each other, for their love and joy is
mutual, Prov. viii , 30, —"I was daily his delight, rejoicing always
before him"—This is the eternal and most perfect and essential
act of the divine nature, wherin the Godhead acts to an infinite
degree and in the most perfect manner possible. The Deity
becomes all act, the Divine essence it self flows out and is as it were
breathed forth in love and joy. So that the Godhead therin
stands forth in yet another manner of subsistence, and there
proceeds the third person in the Trinity, the Holy Spirit, viz.
the deity in act, for there is no other act but the act of the
will.

1. We may learn by the word of God that the Godhead or
the Divine nature and essence does subsist in love. 1 Joh. iv. 8—
" he that loveth not knoweth not God; for God is love." In the
context of which place I think it is plainly intimated to us that
the Holy Spirit is that love, as in the 12 and 13 verses.—" If we
love one another, God dwelleth in us, and his **love** is perfected
in us. Hereby know we that we dwell in him . . . because he
hath given us of his Spirit." 'Tis the same argument in both
verses. In the 12 verse the apostle argues that if we have love
dwelling in us we have God dwelling in us, and in the 13 verse

he clears the force of the argument by this that love is God's Spirit. Seeing we have God's Spirit dwelling in us, we have God dwelling in [in us], supposing it as a thing granted and allowed that God's Spirit is God. 'Tis evident also by this that God's dwelling in us and His love or the love that He hath or exerciseth, being in us, are the same thing. The same is intimated in the same manner in the last verse of the foregoing chapter. The apostle was, in the foregoing verses, speaking of love as a sure sign of sincerity and our acceptance with God, beginning with the 18 verse, and he sums up the argument thus in the last verse, and hereby we know that He abideth in us, by the Spirit which He hath given us.

Again in the 16 verse of this 4 chapter, the Apostle tells us that God is love and he that dwelleth in love dwelleth in God, and God in him, which confirms not only that the divine nature subsists in love, but also that this love is the Spirit, for it is the Spirit of God by which God dwells in His saints, as the Apostle had observed in the 13 verse and as we are abundantly taught in the New Test.

2. The name of the third person in the Trinity, viz. the Holy Spirit confirms it: it naturally expresses the Divine nature as subsisting in pure act and perfect energy, and as flowing out and breathing forth in infinitely sweet and vigorous affection. It is confirmed both by His being called the Spirit and by His being denominated holy. 1. By his being called the Spirit of God: the word Spirit in Scripture when used concerning minds, when it is not put for the spiritual substance or mind it self, is put for the disposition, inclination or temper of the mind: Numb. xiv, 24—" Caleb was of another spirit." Ps. li, 10—" Renew in me a right spirit." Luke ix. 55—" Ye know not what manner of spirit ye are of." S. 1 Thes. v. 23—" I pray God your whole spirit and soul and body." 1 Pet. iii. 4—" The ornament of a meek and quiet spirit." When we read of the spirit of a spirit or mind it is to be thus understood. Eph. iv. 27—" be renewed in the spirit of your mind." So I suppose when we read of the Spirit of God who we are told is a spirit, it is to be understood of

the disposition or temper or affection of the divine mind. If we read or hear of the meek spirit or kind spirit or pious and holy spirit of a man we understand it of his temper: so I suppose we read of the good Spirit and Holy Spirit of God, it is likewise to be understood of God's temper. Now the sum of God's temper or disposition is love, for He is infinite love and, as I observed before, here is no distinction to be made between habit and act, between temper or disposition and exercise. This is the Divine disposition or nature that we are made partakers of, 2 Pet. i. 4, for our partaking or communion with God consists in the communion or partaking of the Holy Ghost.

And it is further confirmed by His being peculiarly denominated holy. The Father and the Son are both infinitely holy and the Holy Ghost can be no holier. But yet the Spirit is especially called holy, which doubtless denotes some peculiarity in the manner in which holiness is attributed to Him. But upon this supposition the matter is easily and clearly explicable. For 1st, it is in the temper or disposition of a mind and its exercise that holiness is immediately seated. A mind is said to be holy from the holiness of its temper and disposition. 2. 'Tis in God's infinite love to Himself that His holiness consists. As all creature holiness is to be resolved into love, as the Scripture teaches us, so doth the holiness of God Himself consist in infinite love to Himself. God's holiness is the infinite beauty and excellence of His nature, and God's excellency consists in His love to Himself as we have observed in[1]

[That the Spirit of God is the very same with holiness (as tis in God, 'tis the holiness of God, and as tis in the Creature, tis the holiness of the creature), appears by John iii. 6, " That which is born of the flesh is flesh; and that which is born of the Spirit is spirit." Here tis very manifest that flesh and spirit are opposed to one another as true contraries, and tis also acknowledged by orthodox divines in general that by the flesh is meant sin or corruption and, therefore by the spirit is meant its contrary, viz. holiness, and that is evidently Christ's meaning, that which is

[1] The next paragraph is a much later insertion.

born of the flesh is corrupt and filthy, but that which is born of
the spirit is holy.]

3. This is very consonant to the office of the Holy Ghost or
His work with respect to creatures, which is threefold, viz. to
quicken, enliven and beautify all things, to sanctify intelligent
[beings] and to comfort and delight them. 1. He quickens and
beautifies all things. So we read that the Spirit of God moved
upon the face of the waters or of the chaos to bring it out of its
confusion into harmony and beauty. So we read, Job xxvi. 13,
that God by His Spirit garnished the heavens. Now whose
office can it be so properly to actuate and enliven all things as
His who is the eternal and essential act and energy of God and
whose office can it be so properly to give all things their sweetness
and beauty as He who is Himself the beauty and joy of the
Creator. 2. 'Tis He that sanctifies created spirits, that is, He
gives them Divine love, for the Scripture teaches us that all holiness and true grace and virtue is resolvable into that as its universal
spring and principle. As it is the office of the person that is God's
idea and understanding to be the light of the world, to communicate understanding, so tis the office of the person that is
God's love to communicate Divine love to the creature. In so
doing, God's spirit or love doth but communicate of it self. Tis
the same love so far as a creature is capable of being made partaker
of it. God's Spirit or His love doth but, as it were, come and
dwell in our hearts and act there as a vital principle, and we
become the living temples of the Holy Ghost, and when men are
regenerated and sanctified, God pours forth of His Spirit upon
them and they have fellowship or, which is the same thing, are
made partakers with the Father and Son of their love, i.e. of their
joy and beauty. Thus the matter is represented in the Gospel—
and this agreable to what was taken notice of before—of the
apostle John, his making love dwelling in us and God's Spirit
dwelling in us the same thing, and the explaining of them one
by another, 1 Joh. iv. 12, 13.

When Christ says to His Father, Joh. xvii. 26—" and I have
declared unto them thy name, and will declare it; that the love

wherewith thou hast loved me may be in them and I in them,"
I can't think of any way that this will appear so easy and intelligible
as upon this hypothesis, viz. that the love with which the Father
loveth the Son is the Holy Spirit, that Christ here concludeth and
sums up His prayer for His disciples with the request that the
Holy Spirit might be in His disciples and so He might be in them
thereby, for Christ dwells in His disciples by His Spirit, as Christ
teaches in John xiv. 16, 17, 18, I will give you another Comforter—even the Spirit of truth—he shall be in you. I will not
leave you comfortless, I will come to you. And the apostle,
Rom. viii. 9, 10, " If so be that the Spirit of God dwell in you.
Now if any man have not the Spirit of Christ, he is none of his.
And if Christ be in you the body is dead."[1]

[Mr. Howe's[2] observation from the v Chap. of Gal. is here
pertinent: Of [from] his Sermons on the Prosperous State of the
Christian Interest before the End of Time, published by Mr. Evans
p. 185. His words are, Walking in the Spirit is directed with a
special eye and reference unto the exercise of this love, as you see
in Gal. v. 14, 15, 16, [in the] verses compared together. All the
law is fulfilled in one word (he means the whole law of the
second table) even in this, Thou shalt love thy neighbour as
thyself. But if ye bite and devour one another (the opposite to
this love or that which follows upon the want of it, or from the
opposite principle) take heed that ye be not consumed one of
another. This I say then (observe the inference) walk in the
Spirit and ye shall not fulfill the lusts of the flesh. To walk in
the Spirit is to walk in the exercise of this love.]

The Scripture seems in many places to speak of love in
christians as if it were the same with the Spirit of God in them,
or at least as the prime and most natural breathing and acting of
the Spirit in the soul. Philip ii. 1—" If there be therefore any
consolation in Christ, if any comfort of love, any fellowship of the
Spirit, if any bowels and mercies, fulfil ye my joy, that ye be

[1] The next paragraph is a later insertion—later than 1726, when this edition
of Howe was issued.
[2] For Howe see footnote on p. 58.—H.

like-minded, having the same love, being of one accord, of one mind." 2 Cor. vi. 6—" by kindness, by the Holy Ghost, by love unfeigned." Rom. xv. 30—" Now I beseech you, brethren, for the Lord Jesus Christ's sake, and for the love of the Spirit." Coloss. i. 8—" who also declared unto us your love in the Spirit." Rom. v. 5 having the love of God "shed abroad in our hearts by the Holy Ghost which is given to us." (See notes on this text). Gal. v. 13, 14, 15, 16—" Use not liberty for an occasion to the flesh, but by love serve one another. For all the law is fulfilled in one word, even in this, Thou shalt love thy neighbour as thy self. But if ye bite and devour one another, take heed that ye be not consumed one of another. This I say then, Walk in the Spirit, and ye shall not fulfil the lust of the flesh." The apostle argues that Christian liberty don't make way for fulfilling the lusts of the flesh in biting and devouring one another and the like, because a principle of love which was the fulfilling of the law would prevent it, and in the 16 verse he asserts the same thing in other words: " This I say then, Walk in the Spirit, and ye shall not fulfil the lust of the flesh."

The third and last office of the Holy Spirit is to comfort and delight the souls of God's people, and thus one of His names is the Comforter, and thus we have the phrase of joy in the Holy Ghost 1 Thes. i. 6—" having received the word in much affliction, with joy of the Holy Ghost." Rom. xiv. 17—" the kingdom of God is righteousness, and peace, and joy in the Holy Ghost." Acts ix. 31—" walking in the fear of the Lord, and in the comfort of the Holy Ghost." But how well doth this agree with the Holy Ghost being God's joy and delight: Acts xiii. 52—" and the disciples were filled with joy, and with the Holy Ghost"—meaning as I suppose that they were filled with spiritual joy.

4. This is confirmed by the symbol of the Holy Ghost, viz. a dove, which is the emblem of love or a lover and is so used in Scripture and especially often so in Solomon's Song, Cant. i. 15—" Behold, thou art fair, my love; behold, thou art fair; thou hast doves' eyes ": i.e. eyes of love, and again iv. 1, the same

words, and v. 12, —" his eyes are as the eyes of doves", and v. 2,
—" my love, my dove," and ii. 14, and vi. 9; and this I believe
to be the reason that the dove alone of all birds (except the sparrow
in the single case of the leprosy) was appointed to be offered in
sacrifice because of its innocency and because it is the emblem of
love, love being the most acceptable sacrifice to God. It was
under this similitude that the Holy Ghost descended from the
Father on Christ at His baptism, signifying the infinite love of
the Father to the Son, who is the true David, or beloved, as we
said before. The same was signified by what was exhibited to
the eye in the appearance there was of the Holy Ghost descending
from the Father to the Son in the shape of a dove, as was signified
by what was exhibited to the eye in the voice there was at the
same time, viz.," This is my beloved Son, in whom I am well
pleased."[1]

[Holy Ghost, love, represented by the symbol of a dove. In
the beginning of Genesis it is said the spirit of God moved upon
the face of the waters. The word translated *moved* in the original
is מְרַחֶפֶת, which as Buxtorf & Grotius observe, properly signifies
the brooding of a dove upon her eggs. See Buxtorf on the
Radix רָחַף and Grotius's truth of the Christian R. B. 1, Sect. 16,
notes, where Grotius observes that the meracheth also signifies
love. See my notes on Gen. i. 2.][2]

5. This is confirmed from the types of the Holy Ghost, and
especially from that type of oil which is often used as a type of the
Holy Ghost and may well represent Divine [love] from its soft,
smooth, flowing and diffusive nature. Oil is from the olive tree
which was of old used to betoken love, peace and friendship.
That was signified by the olive branch with which the dove returned to Noah. It was a token for and a sign of God's love
and favour, after so terrible a manifestation of His displeasure as
the deluge. The olive branch and the dove that brought it were
both the emblems of the same, viz., the love of God. But
especially did the holy anointing oil, the principal type of the

[1] The next paragraph is a late insertion.
[2] The notes referred to can be found in *Works*, vol. ii, p. 677.—H.

Holy Ghost, represent the divine love and delight, by reason of its excellent sweetness and fragrancy. Love is expressly said to be like it in Scripture in the 133 Ps. 20—" Behold how good _____"[1]

[That God's love or his loving kindness is the same with the Holy Ghost seems to be plain by Psalm xxxvi. 7, 8, 9—" How excellent (or how precious, as 'tis in the Hebrew) is thy loving kindness O God! therefore the children of men put their trust under the shadow of thy wings. They shall be abundantly satisfied (in the Hebrew watered) with the fatness of thy house; and thou shalt make them drink of the river of thy pleasures. For with thee is the fountain of life: in thy light shall we see light." Doubtless that precious loving kindness and that fatness of God's house and river of His pleasures and the water of the fountain of life and God's light here spoken [of] are the same thing: by which we learn that the holy anointing oil that was kept in the house of God, which was a type of the Holy Ghost, represented God's love, and that the river of water of life, spoken of in 22 of Revelation, which proceeds out of the throne of God and of the Lamb, which is the same with Ezekiel's vision of living and life-giving water, which is here called the fountain of life and river of God's pleasures, is God's loving-kindness. But Christ himself expressly teaches us that by spiritual fountains and rivers of water of life is meant the Holy Ghost. John iv. 14 and vii. 38, 39.[2] That by the river of God's pleasures here is meant the same thing with that pure river of water of life spoken of in Rev. xxii. 1 will be much confirmed if we compare those verses with Rev. xxi. 23, 24 and chap. xxii. 1, 5 (see the note on chap. xxi. 23, 24). I think if we compare these places and weigh them we cannot doubt but that it is the same happiness that is meant in this Psalm which is spoken of there.]

6. So this well agrees with the similitudes and metaphors that are used about the Holy Ghost in Scripture, such as water, fire, breath, wind, oil, wine, a spring, a river, a being poured out and

[1] The next paragraph is a much later insertion.
[2] What follows is evidently added at a still later time.

shed forth, a being breathed forth. Can there any spirituall
thing be thought, or any thing belonging to any spiritual being
to which such kind of metaphors so naturally agree, as to the
affection of a Spirit. The affection, love or joy, may be said to
flow out as water or to be breathed forth as breath or wind.
But it would [not] sound so well to say that an idea or judgm^t
flows out or is breathed forth. It is no way different to say of the
affection that it is warm, or to compare love to fire, but it would
not seem natural to say the same of perception or reason. It
seems natural enough to say that the soul is poured out in affection
or that love or delight are shed abroad: Tit. iii. 5, 6—"the love of
God is shed abroad in our hearts", but it suits with nothing else
belonging to a spiritual being.

This is that river of water of life spoken of in the 22 of Rev.,
which proceeds from the throne of the Father and the Son, for
the rivers of living water or water of life are the Holy Ghost, by
the same Apostle's own interpretation, John vii. 38, 39; and the
Holy Ghost being the infinite delight and pleasure of God, the
river is called the river of God's pleasures, Ps. xxxvi. 8, not God's
river of pleasures, which I suppose signifies the same as the fatness
of God's house, which they that trust in God shall be watered
with, by which fatness of God's house I suppose is signified
the same thing which oil typifies.

7. It is a confirmation that the Holy Ghost is God's love and
delight, because the saints' communion with God consists in
their partaking of the Holy Ghost. The communion of saints
is twofold: tis their communion with God and communion with
one another: 1 John i. 3—"That ye also may have fellowship with
us: and truly our fellowship is with the Father, and with his Son
Jesus Christ." Communion is a common partaking of good,
either of excellency or happiness, so that when it is said the saints
have communion or fellowship with the Father and with the
Son, the meaning of it is that they partake with the Father and
the Son of their good, which is either their excellency and glory,
(2 Pet. i. 4, ye are made—"partakers of the divine nature"; Heb.
xii. 10. that we might be—"partakers of his holiness"; John xvii.

22, 23—" and the glory which thou hast given me I have given them; that they may be one, even as we are one: I in them and thou in me "); or of their joy and happiness: John.xvii. 13—" that they might have my joy fulfilled in themselves." But the Holy Ghost, being the love and joy of God, is His beauty and happiness, and it is in our partaking of the same Holy Spirit that our communion with God consists: 2 Cor. xiii. 14—" The grace of the Lord Jesus Christ, and the love of God and the communion of the Holy Ghost, be with you all, Amen." They are not different benefits but the same that the apostle here wisheth, viz. the Holy Ghost: in partaking of the Holy Ghost, we possess and enjoy the love and grace of the Father and the Son, for the Holy Ghost is that love and grace, and therefore I suppose it is that in that forementioned place, 1 John i. 3, we are said to have fellowship with the Son and not with the Holy Ghost, because therein consists our fellowship with the Father and the Son, even in partaking with them of the Holy Ghost. In this also eminently consists our communion with the Son that we drink into the same Spirit. This is the common excellency and joy and happiness in which they all are united; tis the bond of perfectness by which they are one in the Father and the Son as the Father is in the Son . . .

8. I can think of no other good account that can be given of the apostle Paul's wishing grace and peace from God the Father and the Lord Jesus Christ in the beginning of his Epistles, without ever mentioning the Holy Ghost,—as we find it thirteen times in his salutations in the beginnings of his Epistles,—But [i.e., except] that the Holy Ghost is Himself love and grace of God the Father and the Lord Jesus Christ; and in his blessing at the end of his second Epistle to the Corinthians where all three persons are mentioned he wishes grace and love from the Son and the Father [except that], in the communion or the partaking of the Holy Ghost, the blessing from the Father and the Son is the Holy Ghost. But the blessing from the Holy Ghost is Himself, the communication of Himself. John xiv. 21, 23, Christ promises that He and the Father will love believers, but no mention is made of the Holy Ghost, and the love of Christ and the love of the

Father are often distinctly mentioned, but never any mention of the Holy Ghost's love.[1]

[This I suppose to be the reason why we have never any account of the Holy Ghost's loving either the Father or the Son, or of the Son's or the Father's loving the Holy Ghost, or of the Holy Ghost's loving the saints, tho' these things are so often predicated of both the other persons.]

And this I suppose to be that blessed Trinity that we read of in the Holy Scriptures. The Father is the deity subsisting in the prime, unoriginated and most absolute manner, or the deity in its direct existence. The Son is the deity generated by God's understanding, or having an idea of Himself and subsisting in that idea. The Holy Ghost is the deity subsisting in act, or the divine essence flowing out and breathed forth in God's infinite love to and delight in Himself. And I believe the whole Divine essence does truly and distinctly subsist both in the Divine idea and Divine love, and that each of them are properly distinct persons.

And it confirms me in it that this is the true Trinity because reason is sufficient to tell us that there must be these distinctions in the deity, viz., of God (absolutely considered), and the idea of God, and love and delight, and there are no other real distinctions in God that can be thought. There are but these three distinct real things in God. Whatsoever else can be mentioned in God are nothing but meer modes or relations of existence. There are His attributes of infinity, eternity and immortality; they are meer modes of existence. There is God's understanding, His wisdom and omniscience that we have shewn to be the same with His idea. There is God's will, but this is not really distinguished from His love, but is the same but only with a different relation. As the sum of God's understanding consists in His having an idea of Himself, so the sum of His will or inclination consists in His loving Himself, as we have already observed. There is God's power or ability to bring things to pass. But this is not really distinct from His understanding and will; it is the same but only with the relation they have to those effects that are,

[1] The next paragraph is a later insertion.

or are to be produced. There is God's holiness, but this is the same, as we have shewn in what we have said of the nature of excellency, with His love to Himself. There is God's justice, which is not really distinct from His holiness. There are the attributes of goodness, mercy and grace, but these are but the overflowing of God's infinite love. The sum of all God's love is His love to Himself. These three, God, and the idea of God, and the inclination, affection and love of God, must be conceived as really distinct. But as for all these other things of extent, duration, being with or without change, ability to do, they are not distinct real things even in created spirits but only meer modes and relations. So that our natural reason is sufficient to tell us that there are these three in God, and we can think of no more.

It is a maxim amongst divines that everything that is in God is God which must be understood of real attributes and not of meer modalities. If a man should tell me that the immutability of God is God or that the omnipresence of God and authority of God, is God, I should not be able to think of any rational meaning of what he said. It hardly sounds to me proper to say that God's being without change is God, or that God's being everywhere is God, or that God's having a right of government over creatures is God. But if it be meant that the real attributes of God, viz. His understanding and love are God, then what we have said may in some measure explain how it is so, for deity subsists in them distinctly; so they are distinct Divine persons. We find no other attributes of which it is said that they are God in Scripture or that God is they, but Λόγος and Ἀγάπη, the reason and the love of God. John i. 1, and 1 John iv. 8, 16. Indeed it is said that God is light, 1 John i. 5, but what can we understand by Divine light different from the divine reason or understanding? The same apostle tells us that Christ is the true light, John i. 9, and the apostle Paul tells us that he is the effulgence of the Father's glory, Heb. i. 3.[1]

[This is that light that the Holy Ghost in the prophet Daniel says dwells with God, Dan. ii. 22—" and the light dwelleth with

[1] The next paragraph is inserted later.

him,"—the same with that word or reason that the Apostle John says, 1 chap. of his Gospel, was with God and was God, that he there says is the true light, and speaks much of, vide that chapter, v. 4, 5, 7, 8, 9. This is that wisdom that says in the 8 of Prov., 30 verse, that he was by God as one brought up with Him. This is the light with respect to which especially God the Father may be called the Father of lights.]

One of the principal objections that I can think of against what has been supposed is concerning the personality of the Holy Ghost—that this scheme of things don't seem well to consist with [the fact] that a person is that which hath understanding and will. If the three in the Godhead are persons they doubtless each of them have understanding, but this makes the understanding one distinct person and love another. How therefore can this love be said to have understanding? (Here I would observe that divines have not been wont to suppose that these three had three distinct understandings, but all one and the same understanding). In order to clear up this matter let it be considered that the whole Divine office is supposed truly and properly to subsist in each of these three, viz., God and His understanding and love, and that there is such a wonderfull union between them that they are, after an ineffable and inconceivable manner, one in another, so that one hath another and they have communion in one another and are as it were predicable one of another; as Christ said of Himself and the Father, I am in the Father and the Father in me, so may it be said concerning all the persons in the Trinity, the Father is in the Son and the Son in the Father, the Holy Ghost is in the Father, and the Father in the Holy Ghost, the Holy Ghost is in the Son and the Son in the Holy Ghost, and the Father understands because the Son who is the divine understanding is in Him, the Father loves because the Holy Ghost is in Him, so the Son loves because the Holy Ghost is in Him and proceeds from Him, so the Holy Ghost or the divine essence subsisting is divine, but understands because the Son the divine idea is in Him. Understanding may be predicated of this love because it is the love of the understanding both objectively and subjectively.

God loves the understanding and that understanding also flows out in love so that the divine understanding is in the deity subsisting in love. It is not a blind love. Even in creatures there is consciousness included in the very nature of the will or act of the soul, and tho' perhaps not so that it can so properly be said that it is a seeing or understanding will, yet it may truly and properly be said so in God, by reason of God's infinitely more perfect manner of acting so that the whole Divine essence flows out and subsists in this act, and the Son is in the Holy Spirit tho' it don't proceed from Him by reason [of the fact] that the understanding must be considered as prior in the order of nature to the will or love or act, both in creatures and in the Creator. The understanding is so in the Spirit that the Spirit may be said to know, as the Spirit of God is truly and perfectly said to know and to search all things, even the deep things of God.[1]

[All the three are persons for they all have understanding and will. There is understanding and will in the Father, as the Son and the Holy Ghost are in Him and proceed from Him. There is understanding and will in the Son, as He is understanding and as the Holy Ghost is in Him and proceeds from Him. There is understanding and will in the Holy Ghost as He is the divine will and as the Son is in Him. Nor is it to be looked upon as a strange and unreasonable figment that the persons should be said to have an understanding or love by another person's being in them, for we have Scripture ground to conclude so concerning the Father's having wisd. and understanding or reason that it is by the Son's being in Him; because we are there informed that He is the wisd. and reason and truth of God and hereby God is wise by His own wisdom being in Him. Understanding and wisdom is in the Father as the Son is in Him and proceeds from Him. Understanding is in the Holy Ghost because the Son is in Him, not as proceeding from Him but as flowing out of Him.]

But I don't pretend fully to explain how these things are and I am sensible a hundred other objections may be made and puzzling doubts and questions raised that I can't solve. I am far

[1] The next paragraph is a later insertion.

from pretending to explaining the Trinity so as to render it no longer a mystery. I think it to be the highest and deepest of all Divine mysteries still, notwithstanding anything that I have said or conceived about it. I don't intend to explain the Trinity. But Scripture with reason may lead to say something further of it than has been wont to be said, tho' there are still left many things pertaining to it incomprehensible. It seems to me that what I have here supposed concerning the Trinity is exceeding analogous to the gospel scheme and agreeable to the tenour of the whole New Testament and abundantly illustrative of gospel doctrines, as might be particularly shewn, would it not exceedingly lengthen out this discourse.

I shall only now briefly observe that many things that have been wont to be said by orthodox divines about the Trinity are hereby illustrated. Hereby we see how the Father is the fountion of the Godhead, and why when He is spoken of in Scripture He is so often, without any addition or distinction, called God, which has led some to think that He only was truly and properly God. Hereby we may see why in the oeconomy of the persons of the Trinity the Father should sustain the dignity of the deity, that the Father should have it as His office to uphold and maintain the rights of the Godhead and should be God not only by essence but, as it were, by His oeconomical office. Hereby is illustrated the doctrine of the Holy Ghost. Proceeding [from] both the Father and the Son. Hereby we see how that it is possible for the Son to be begotten by the Father and the Holy Ghost to proceed from the Father and Son, and yet that all the persons should be coeternal. Hereby we may more clearly understand the equality of the persons among themselves, and that they are every way equal in the society or family of the three. They are equal in honour: besides the honour which is common to 'em all, viz. that they are all God, each has His peculiar honour in the society or family. They are equal not only in essence, but the Father's honour is that He is, as it were, the author of perfect and infinite wisdom. The Son's honour is that He is that perfect and divine wisdom itself the excellency of which is that from whence arises the honour of being the author or generator of it. The honour of the Father and the Son is that they are infinitely excellent, or that from them infinite excellency proceeds; but the honour of the Holy Ghost is equal for He is that divine excellency and beauty itself. Tis the honour of the Father and the Son that they are infinitely holy and are the fountain of holiness, but the honour of the Holy Ghost is that holiness itself. The honour of the Father and the Son is [that] they are infinitely happy and are the original and fountain of happiness, and the honour of the Holy Ghost is equal for He is infinite happiness and joy itself. The honour of the Father is that He is the fountain of the deity as He from whom proceed both the Divine wisdom and also excellency and happiness. The honour of the Son is equal for He is Himself the Divine wisdom and is He from whom proceeds the Divine excellency and happiness, and the honour of the Holy Ghost is equal for He is the beauty and happiness of both the other persons.

By this also we may fully understand the equality of each person's concern in the work of redemption, and the equality of the redeemeds' concern with them and dependence upon them, and the equality and honour and praise due to each of them. Glory belongs to the Father and the Son that they so greatly loved the world: to the Father that He so loved that He gave His only begotten Son: to the Son that He so loved the world as to give up Himself. But there is equal glory due to the Holy Ghost, for He is that love of the Father and the Son to the world. Just so much as the two first Persons glorify themselves by showing the astonishing greatness of their love and grace, just so much is that wonderful love and grace glorified who is the Holy Ghost. It shows the infinite dignity and excellency of the Father that the Son so delighted and prized His honour and glory that He stooped infinitely low rather than [that] men's salvation should be to the injury of that honour and glory. It showed the infinite excellency and worth of the Son that the Father so delighted in Him that for His sake He was ready to quit His anger and receive into favour those that had [deserved?] infinitely ill at His hands. And what was done shews how great the excellency and worth of the Holy Ghost who is that delight which the Father and the Son have in each other: it shows it to be infinite. So great as the worth of a thing delighted in is to any one, so great is the worth of that delight and joy itself which he has in it.

Our dependence is equally upon each in this office. The Father appoints and provides the Redeemer, and Himself accepts the price and grants the thing purchased; the Son is the Redeemer by offering Himself and is the price; and the Holy Ghost immediately communicates to us the thing purchased by communicating Himself, and He is the thing purchased. The sum of all that Christ purchased for men was the Holy Ghost: Gal. iii. 13. 14—" He was made a curse for us—that we might receive the promise of the Spirit through faith." What Christ purchased for us was that we have communion with God [which] in His good, which consists in partaking of the Holy Ghost: as we have shown, all the blessedness of the redeemed consists in their partaking of Christ's fullness, which consists in partaking of that Spirit which is given not by measure unto Him: the oil that is poured on the Head of the Church runs down to the members of His body and to the skirts of His garment, Ps. cxxxiii. 2. Christ purchased for us that we should have the favour of God and might enjoy His love, but His love is the Holy Ghost. Christ purchased for us true spiritual excellency, grace and holiness, the sum of which is love to God, which is [nothing] but the indwelling of the Holy Ghost in the heart. Christ purchased for us spiritual joy and comfort, which is in a participation of God's joy and happiness, which joy and happiness is the Holy Ghost, as we have shewn. The Holy Ghost is the sum of all good things. Good things and the Holy Spirit are synonymous expressions in Scripture: Luke xi. 13—" how much more shall your heavenly Father give the Holy Spirit to them that ask him." The sum of all spiritual good which the finite have in this world is that spring of living water within them which we read of, John iv. 10, etc., and those rivers of living water flowing out of them which we read of, John vii. 38, 39, which we are there told means the Holy Ghost; and the sum of all happiness in the other world is that river of water of life which proceeds out of the throne of God and the Lamb, which we read of, Rev. xxii. 1, which is the river of God's pleasures and is the Holy Ghost and therefore the sum of the Gospel invitation to come and take the water of life, verse 17. The Holy Ghost is the purchased possession and inheritance of the saints, as appears because that little of it which the saints have in this world is said to be the ernest of that purchased inheritance, Eph. i. 14. 2 Cor. i. 22 and v. 5, 'tis an ernest of that which we are to have a fullness of hereafter. The Holy Ghost is the great subject of all gospel promises and therefore is called the Spirit of promise, Eph. i. 13. This is called the promise of the Father, Luke xxiv. 49, and the like in other places.[1] [If the Holy Ghost be a comprehension of all good things promised in the Gospel, we may easily see the force of the apostle's arguing, Gal. iii. 2—" This only would I learn of you, received ye the Spirit by the works of the law or by the hearing of faith?"] So that 'tis God of whom our good is purchased and 'tis God that purchases it and tis God also that is the thing purchased. Thus all our good things are of God and through God and in God, as we read in Rom. xi. 36 —" for of him, and through him, and to him, (or in him as εἰς is rendered, 1 Cor. viii. 6) are all things: to whom be glory forever." All our good is of God the Father, 'tis all through God the Son, and all is in the Holy Ghost, as He is Himself all our good. God is Himself the portion and purchased inheritance of His people. Thus God is the Alpha and Omega in this affair of Redemption. If we suppose no more than used to be supposed about the Holy Ghost the concern of the Holy Ghost in the work of redemption is not equal with the Father's and the Son's, nor is there an equal part of the glory of this work belonging to him: meerly to apply to us or immediately to give or hand to us the blessing purchased, after it was purchased, as subservient to the other two persons, is but a little thing [compared] to the purchasing of it by the paying an infinite price, by Christ offering up Himself in sacrifice to procure it, and 'tis but a little thing to God the Father's giving

---

[1] The next sentence is added as a later footnote.

His infinitely dear Son to be a sacrifice for us and upon His purchase to afford to us all the blessings of His purchased. But according to this there is an equality. To be the love of God to the world is as much as for the Father and the Son to do so much from love to the world, and to be the thing purchased was so much as to be the price. The price and the thing bought with that price are equal. And 'tis as much as to afford the thing purchased, for the glory that belongs to Him that affords the thing purchased arises from the worth of that thing that He affords and therefore 'tis the same glory and an equal glory; the glory of the thing itself is its worth and that is also the glory of Him that affords it.

There are two more eminent and remarkable images of the Trinity among the creatures. The one is in the spiritual creation, the soul of man. There is the mind, and the understanding or idea and the spirit of the mind as it is called in Scripture i.e. the disp[osition], the will or affection. The other is in the visible creation viz. the sun. The Father is as the substance of the sun. (By substance I don't mean in a philosophical sense, but the sun as to its internal constitution.) The Son is as the brightness and glory of the disk of the sun or that bright and glorious form under which it appears to our eyes. The Holy Ghost is the action of the sun which is within the sun in its intestine heat, and, being diffusive, enlightens, warms, enlivens and comforts the world. The Spirit, as it is God's infinite love to Himself and happiness in Himself, is as the internal heat of the sun, but, as it is that by which God communicates Himself, it is as the emanation of the sun's action, or the emitted beams of the sun.

The various sorts of rays of the sun and their beautiful colours do well represent the Spirit.[1] They well [represent the love and grace of God and were made use of for this purpose in the rainbow after the flood and I suppose also in that rainbow that was seen round about the throne by Ezekiel: Ezek i.28, Rev. iv. 3 and round the head of Christ by John, Rev. x. 1], or the amiable excellency of God and the various beautiful graces and virtues of

[1] The following sentence was inserted later.

the Spirit. These beautiful colours of the sunbeams we find made use of in Scripture for this purpose, viz. to represent the graces of the Spirit, as Ps. lxviii verse 13—" Tho ye have lien among the pots, yet shall ye be as the wings of a dove covered with silver, and her feathers with yellow gold", i.e. like the light reflected in various beautiful colours from the feathers of a dove, which colours represent the graces of the heavenly dove. The same I suppose is signified by the various beautiful colours reflected from the precious stones of the breastplate, and that these spiritual ornaments of the Church are what are represented by the various colours of the foundation and gates of the new Jerusalem, Rev. xxi. and Isaiah liv. 11 etc.—and the stones of the temple, 1 Chron. xxix, 2; and I believe the variety there is in the rays of the sun and their beautiful colours was designed by the Creator for this very purpose, and indeed that the whole visible creation which is but the shadow of being is so made and ordered by God as to typify and represent spiritual things, for which I could give many reasons.[1] [I don't propose this meerly as an hypothesis but as a part of divine truth sufficiently and fully ascertained by the revelation God has made in the Holy Scriptures.][2]

[I am sensible what kind of objections many will be ready to make against what has been said, what difficulties will be immediately found, how can this be? and how can that be?

I am far from affording this as any explication of this mystery, that unfolds and renews the mysteriousness and incomprehensibleness of it, for I am sensible that however by what has been said some difficulties are lessened, others that are new appear, and the number of those things that appear mysterious, wonderful and incomprehensible, is increased by it. I offer it only as a farther manifestation of what of divine truth the Word of God exhibits to the view of our minds concerning this great mystery. I think the Word of God teaches us more things concerning it to be believed by us than have been generally believed, and that it

---

[1] The next sentence is a later addition.
[2] The original treatise appears to end here; what follows is independently written later, on another sheet.

exhibits many things concerning it exceeding [*i.e.*, more] glorious and wonderful than have been taken notice of; yea, that it reveals or exhibits many more wonderful mysteries than those which have been taken notice of; which mysteries that have been over-valued are incomprehensible things and yet have been exhibited in the Word of God, tho they are an addition to the number of mysteries that are in it. No wonder that the more things we are told concerning that which is so infinitely above our reach, the number of visible mysteries increases. When we tell a child a little concerning God he has not an hundredth part so many mysteries in view on the nature and attributes of God and His works of creation and providence as one that is told much concerning God in a divinity school; and yet he knows much more about God and has a much clearer understanding of things of divinity and is able more clearly to explicate some things that were dark and very unintelligible to him. I humbly apprehend that the things that have been observed increase the number of visible mysteries in the Godhead in no other manner than as by them we perceive that God has told us much more about it then was before generally observed. Under the Old Testament the Church of God were not told near so much about the Trinity as they are now. But what the New Testament has revealed, tho' it has more opened to our view the nature of God, yet it has increased the number of visible mysteries and they thus appear to us exceeding wonderfull and incomprehensible. And so also it has come to pass in the Churches, being told [*i.e.*, that the Churches are told] more about the incarnation and the satisfaction of Christ and other gospel doctrines. 'Tis so not only in divine things but natural things. He that looks on a plant, or the parts of the bodies of animals, or any other works of nature, at a great distance where he has but an obscure sight of it, may see something in it wonderfull and beyond his comprehension, but he that is near to it and views them narrowly indeed understands more about them, has a clearer and distinct sight of them, and yet the number of things that are wonderfull and mysterious in them that appear to him are much more than before, and, if he views them with a microscope, the number of the wonders that he sees will be much increased still, but yet the microscope gives him more of a true knowledge concerning them.]

God is never said to love the Holy Ghost, nor are any epithets that betoken love any where given to Him, tho' so many are ascribed to the Son, as God's elect, the beloved, He in whom God's soul delighteth, He in whom He is well pleased etc.— Yea such epithets seem to be ascribed to the Son as tho'He were the object of love exclusive of all other persons, as tho'there were no person whatsoever to share the love of the Father with the Son. To this purpose evidently He is called God's only begotten Son, at the time that it is added, In whom He is well pleased. There is nothing in Scripture that speaks of any acceptance of the Holy Ghost, or any reward or any mutual friendship between the Holy Ghost and either of the other persons, or any command to love the Holy Ghost or to delight in or have any complacence in, tho' such commands are so frequent with respect to the other persons.

The Son of God] Agreable to the Son of God's being the wisdom of understanding of God is that Zech. iii, 9, read—" For behold the stone that I have laid before Joshua; upon one stone shall be seven eyes. This stone is the Messiah (See observations on the place in my discourse on the prophecies of the Messiah: Miscel. B. 6.) By these eyes is represented God's understanding, [as shewn] by the explanation which God Himself gives of it in the next chap. verse 10. These seven are the eyes of the Lord which run to and fro through the whole earth. The seven eyes, being by a wonderfull work of God graven on the stone, a thing in itself very far from sight, represents the incarnation of Christ in uniteing the logos or wisdom of God to that which is in it self so weak and blind and infinitely far from divinity as the human nature. The same again is represented, Rev. v. 6—" And I beheld, and lo, in the midst of the throne and of the four beasts, and in the midst of the elders, stood a Lamb as it had been slain, having seven horns and seven eyes, which are the seven Spirits of God." The plain allusion here to that other place in Zechary shews that the stone there spoken of, with seven eyes, is the Messiah, that elsewhere is often called a stone. And whereas [*i.e.*, with reason] these seven eyes are said to be the seven spirits of God i.e. the perfect and alsufficient Spirit of God, for 'tis by the Holy Spirit that the Divine nature and the Divine logos or understanding or wisdom is united to the human nature.

That in Rom. v. 5, the love of God is shed abroad in our hearts by the Holy Ghost etc. in the original is the love of God is poured out into our hearts by the Holy Ghost which is given to us; so that the same representation is made of the manner of communicating it that is made from time to time to signify the manner of communicating the Spirit of God Himself and the same expression used to signify it. The love of God is not said to be poured out into our hearts, in any propriety [of speech], any other way than as the Holy Spirit which is the love of God is poured out into our hearts, and it seems to be intimated that it is this way that the love of God is poured out into our hearts by the words annexed, *by the Holy Ghost* which is given to us.

Holy Ghost. These two texts illustrate one the other: Cant. i. 4—" we will remember thy love more than wine," and Eph. v. 18—" Be not drunk with wine ... but be filled with the Spirit."

That knowledge or understanding in God which we must conceive of as first is His knowledge of every thing possible. That love which must be this knowledge is what we must conceive of as belonging to the essence of the Godhead in its first subsistence. Then comes a reflex act of knowledge and His viewing Himself and knowing Himself and so knowing His own knowledge and so the Son is begotten. There is such a thing in God as knowledge of knowledge, an idea of an idea. Which can be nothing else than the idea or knowledge repeated.

The world was made for the Son of God especially. For God made the world for Himself from love to Himself; but God loves Himself only in a reflex act. He views Himself and so loves Himself, so He makes the world for Himself viewed and reflected on, and that is the same with Himself repeated or begotten in His own idea, and that is His Son. When God considers of making any thing for Himself He presents Himself before Himself and views Himself as His end, and that viewing Himself is the same as reflecting on Himself or having an idea of Himself, and to make the world for the Godhead thus viewd and understood is to make the world for the Godhead begotten and that is to make the world for the Son of God.

The love of God as it flows forth ad extra is wholly determined and directed by Divine wisdom, so that those only are the objects of it that Divine wisdom chuses, so that the creation of the world is to gratify Divine love as that is exercised by divine wisdom. But Christ is Divine wisdom, so that the world is made to gratify Divine love as exercised by Christ or to gratify the love that is in Christ's heart to provide a spouse for Christ. Those creatures which wisdom chuses for the object of Divine love are Christ's elect spouse and especially those elect creatures that wisdom chiefly pitches upon and makes the end of the rest of creatures.